HOT RODS

Alan Mayes

motorbooks

First published in 2010 by Motorbooks, an imprint of MBI Publishing Company, 400 First Avenue North, Suite 300, Minneapolis, MN 55401 USA

Motorbooks titles are also available at discounts in bulk quantity for industrial or sales-promotional use. For details write to Special Sales Manager at MBI Publishing Company, 400 First Avenue North, Suite 300, Minneapolis, MN 55401 USA.

To find out more about our books, visit us online at www.motorbooks.com.

ISBN-13: 978-0-7603-3861-2

Editor: Melinda Keefe
Design Manager: John Sticha
Series designed by: Laura Rades
Layout by: Kazuko Collins

Printed in China

Cover photo © Car Culture/Getty Images
Back cover photo, bottom © Jimmy Faris
Photo on page 4 © John Jackson

Library of Congress Cataloging-in-Publication Data
Mayes, Alan.
Hot rods / Alan Mayes.
    p. cm.
Includes index.
ISBN 978-0-7603-3861-2 (sb w/ flaps : alk. paper)
1. Hot rods--United States--History. 2. Hot rods--United States--Pictorial works. I. Title.
TL236.3.M37 2010
629.228'60973--dc22
                            2010003520

CONTENTS

ACKNOWLEDGMENTS

This book would not have been possible without the assistance of some good friends and photographers. I am deeply indebted to the owners and builders of all of the included cars, as well as these people listed below who graciously loaned me their photos, as well as the information about the cars.

Eric Corlay

Jack Criswell

Max Duryea

Jimmy Faris

Tom Gomez

Aaron Hagar

John Jackson

Roger Jetter

Chadly Johnson

Charlie Lecach

Jean-Sylvain Marchessou

Anna Marco

Craig Mayes

David W. Miller

Carrol Schenck

Gary Vahling

Mitzi Valenzuela

Roy Varga

INTRODUCTION

Hot rods are cars made by and for a chosen few. Not everyone has the personality or stamina to drive a hot rod. They are extremely basic; little more than wheels, an engine, a steering wheel, and a seat plus the bare necessities required to hold those elements together in a functional vehicle. Or, in some cases, a dysfunctional vehicle. Most of them are noisy, they often rattle, they may be dusty, and sometimes they stink of gas and oil and exhaust fumes. The prim and proper will not like them.

Hot rods belong to America. They were invented in America, they were developed by Americans, utilizing American cars and American ingenuity. There are hot rods in other countries, of course, but nearly all of them are built from American cars with

American engines and American speed equipment. Even in Japan, New Zealand, France, or Sweden, hot rods are American. No Toyotas, no Volvos, no Peugeots; just Fords, Chevys, Plymouths, and Willys, with few exceptions.

Hot rods were the brainchildren of American servicemen returning from World War II. These were restless men with extra money, a lot of time on their hands, and a quest for speed and power fueled by their experiences in war. Well, that's the popular story anyway.

That story doesn't explain all the hot rodded Model Ts that were running on tracks and back roads in the 1920s and 1930s. Nor does it explain the 1930 Ford roadster in Chapter 1 that has been a hot rod since 1936, nine years before the end of World War II (and five years before the United States even entered the war). The truth is, hot rods have been around in some form almost since the automobile's birth.

Ever hear of a guy named Henry Ford? He and other early automotive pioneers were building hot rods—stripped-down versions of their production cars—as early as 1901 in order to create publicity and raise funds for their fledgling car companies. Those were the beginnings of hot rods, and early hot rodders followed in that vein.

The glamorous, sunny, and warm climate of Southern California was the original hot bed of hot rodding. The area's dry lake beds offered miles of wide-open, flat spaces where hot rodders could test both their mettle and their metal. Drivers worked on their cars during the week and drove them back and forth to work too. Then on the weekend, they'd drive out to the dry lakes and test the week's work. On Sunday, after all the racing was done, they'd go back home and start the whole cycle again.

California was only one of many hot rod hubs, though. Rodders in the East and Midwest were doing the same things but testing their cars on the beaches of Florida and South Carolina or on Michigan's frozen lakes or Kentucky's back roads. No matter where they were, the procedures and results were the same.

Stripping the non-critical parts—fenders, running boards, extra seats, tops on roadsters, bumpers—was the same as buying horsepower except that it was free for a few hours of labor spent unbolting all those heavy parts. Taking off 10 percent of the car's weight was the equivalent to raising the horsepower by 10 percent. Lowering the weight not only made the car go faster, it made it handle better, and it stopped better too because the brakes were slowing down a smaller mass. Of course that mass was capable of going faster, so it might have been a tradeoff!

More horsepower was added by hopping up the existing engine or swapping in a more powerful one from a different car. Enterprising hot rodders like Ed Iskenderian, Dean Moon, Fred Offenhauser, Eddie Meyer, and Vic Edelbrock Sr. established well-known businesses by experimenting with procedures and components on their own cars and then reproducing the resultant parts and selling them to other hot rodders. Others like "Honest Charley" Card, Ed Almquist, and Gene Winfield raced their own cars and sold other hot rodders' parts out of their trunks to pay for their own racing habits.

Most guys did their own work and helped their buddies do the same. Early hot rod clubs, some of which have survived 60 years, were formed around this camaraderie. They shared tools, knowledge, and skills to help fellow club members accomplish the goal of all hot rodders: to go as fast as possible with what they have.

That's what hot rodding is about, and that's what most of the cars in this book reflect, though with a few twists. This book is divided into three chapters, each with a different variation on the overall genus of the hot rod: traditional hot rods, show rods, and rat rods. You will find some fine examples of each. It's important to note that no two are even remotely alike, yet each is a hot rod that reflects its owner's taste and his or her vision of what a hot rod should be.

Four cars are restored, significant, historical cars; one is a clone of a very famous show rod; and one traditional rod is not what it seems. These cars are hot rods built and owned by people who have the spirit of the early hot rodders, and, as such, they reflect the history and purpose of those early days.

CHAPTER 1

TRADITIONAL HOT RODS

The name "traditional hot rod" has been bandied about quite a bit lately, and not necessarily with a lot of clarity. It's used to describe everything from old survivor hot rods from the early days to fiberglass street rods to rat rods to '57 Chevys. Obviously, unless "traditional hot rod" is a vague term with all the meaning of "car," those are not all traditional hot rods. Also obvious is that there is no "official" meaning of the term, but rather a generally accepted understanding shared by a majority of hot rodders.

Plainly put, a traditional hot rod transcends time frames. Even looking at its details closely, it will be difficult or impossible to discern exactly when it was built. That's because it will have a timeless design and execution that ignores all fads and short-lived trends.

The hot rods in this first chapter fit into that definition. Were they built in 1947, 1967, or 1987, or were they finished last month? Their appearance gives no clue. A Model A roadster with a 1938 Ford flathead looks the same no matter when it was built. The transmission is hidden under the floor, so is it a 1939 Ford box with Zephyr gears or is it an S-10 five-speed overdrive? A 1956 Chevy small-block engine block looks the same as a new small-block crate engine. Put an Edelbrock three-deuce manifold and three Stromberg carbs on it and try to put a date on it. If it was done right, the dating is difficult and often impossible.

Traditional hot rods, as a matter of definition, follow *tradition—* specifically the traditions set forth by early hot rodders. Those were pretty simple. Basically, they took an early car, usually a roadster or coupe, and stripped it of every unnecessary part that didn't make it go, stop, or steer. Then they did everything in their power (and budget) to make the car go as fast as it would go in a straight line or on a curvy road.

"Period correct" is another term that's been overused lately, as though the use of that term justifies a car that is ugly or faddish. Not all popular styles from over the decades deserve to be preserved or even remembered, other than as a lesson never to be repeated. There are reasons that some of those styles fell out of favor, and not a minute too soon, either. They were hideous!

Classic good looks and taste are timeless, though. That's why these hot rods have no wooden running boards, shag carpets, pink velour interiors, 24-inch "donk" wheels, or any of that sort of tasteless kitsch. Every car in this chapter is period correct except for some added features as nods to safety or drivability, yet most give little hint of their construction dates. That's because a traditional hot rod will always be in style, and the style doesn't change much. Timeless and classy. Each of these is period correct because it's correct, period.

Look at the cars in this chapter to see a good cross-section of what a traditional hot rod

should look like. One has been a hot rod since 1936, and a couple were finished in 2008. The rest fit somewhere in between. Some people (who don't know much about hot rods) would call a few of these cars rat rods because they have faded paint or are in primer. None of these is a rat rod, though. Traditional hot rods aren't likely to look pristine for the simple fact that the owner drives them. That doesn't make them rat rods. Rat rods are a whole different animal. No pun intended. You want rat rods? See Chapter 3.

With one or two exceptions, most of these cars seldom, if ever, see a trailer, and they are driven quite a bit because their owners built them for that purpose. They rightly assume that it is pointless to build a hot rod that is not going to be driven. Where's the fun in that?

Dave Kinnaman of Alexandria, Indiana, built this 1929 Model A coupe twice. He built it as a street rod in the early 1990s, and then when the owner of the car died, it sat in Dave's barn for about 15 years. He decided to rebuild it as a traditional 1950s-style hot rod, and that's when the author stumbled upon it. He and Kinnaman struck a deal, and the car was finished.

Kinnaman certainly knows how to build cars the right way—traditional, safe, road-worthy, and in good taste. Chopped 3 inches and channeled 4 inches, and with a 1950 Merc flattie and a '40 Ford drivetrain otherwise (from a running '40 chassis), the car is extremely traditional in appearance. It even runs a 1940 Ford column with three on the tree.

You'll note that no visible component appears newer than 1955 (the emergency brake from a '55 Chevy), though some are reproductions of vintage parts (Speedway Motors beehive oil filter, Ron Francis turn-signal switch). Tires are bias-ply big and little (6.00-15 and 8.20-15) B. F. Goodrich blackwalls from Coker Tire. Under the floor is a dual master cylinder to feed juice safely to the rebuilt '40 Ford brakes. Tucked neatly under the dashboard is a Bare Bonz wiring panel from Ron Francis Wiring.

The car was finished in time to debut at the 2008 Indianapolis World of Wheels. One of America's top pinstripers, Darin Allen (Killer Designs by Darin), pinstriped the A-bone at the show while show attendees watched.

1929 FORD COUPE

Owner: Alan Mayes
Builder: Dave Kinnaman
Engine: 1950 Mercury flathead
Photographer: Alan Mayes

Did You Know?

Although it looks like tinted primer, the paint on this car is "Speed Blue" Hot Rod Flatz urethane enamel from Kustom Shop. It comes with the flattener already mixed in, which gives the popular flat appearance but is as durable as regular urethane. The pinstriping was done in flat Kustom Shop striping enamel.

The owner of this 1932 Ford (a.k.a. "Deuce") is Jackie Howerton, former race car driver and now a fabricator in Indianapolis, Indiana. Joe Mac from Ford Parts Obsolete owned the car for 35 years, and it has been a hot rod since at least the 1940s.

Befitting a hot rod owned by a race car guy, this roadster is powered by a '46 Mercury flathead running 296 cubic inches. Dual Stromberg carbs sit atop a polished Eddie Meyer manifold. It also uses a Potvin cam, Evans heads, and a Harmon Collins ignition. Fenton cast-iron headers and dual Smithy's mufflers sing the sweet flathead song. The 1939 Ford transmission is stuffed with Lincoln Zephyr gears, a common early hot rodding practice.

A Halibrand quick-change rear end hangs off a Model A spring. The brakes are from a '48 Ford, and the wheels are triple pinstriped 16-inch steel versions with 5.25-inch front tires and 7.00-inch rear.

The roadster wears an extremely rare Duke Hallock windshield. Hallock made several Model A roadster windshields back in the day, which were cast in a high school shop foundry. This is the only one that was made for a Deuce, however. Jackie Howerton's '32 has a reworked dash with real Auburn gages and an original Bell Racing steering wheel on a Ford F-100 column. The seats are upholstered in brown leather.

Jackie Howerton's roadster is one of those cars with a special appeal. It looks like it's not quite finished, but Howerton says otherwise.

1932 FORD ROADSTER

Owner: Jackie Howerton
Builder: Joe Mac
Engine: 1946 Mercury flathead
Photographer: Alan Mayes

Did You Know?

The previous owner of this car was Nick Alexander, son of the late actor Ben Alexander, one of the stars of the original *Dragnet* TV series. Ben owned a Ford dealership in San Francisco at one time, and a diecast license-plate frame from the dealership is still on this car.

Dave Kinnaman's wife, Vickie, put up with a lot of years of going to far-away rod runs and long-distance vacations in their 1929 Ford roadster. She was really happy when Dave decided to build this 1940 Ford sedan. The promise of roll-up windows, heat, air conditioning, and even a back seat put a smile on her face every time they talked about it. She was really smiling when the car was done and they were actually using it.

Dave has been a fan of Bob McCoy's iconic '40 Ford sedan hot rod since he first spotted it in the *1958 Hot Rod Annual*. When he decided to build a '40 for himself, he

1940 FORD SEDAN

Owner: Mike Miraglia
Builder: Dave Kinnaman
Engine: 1969 Chevy 350
Photographer: Craig Mayes

patterned it after McCoy's, right down to the duplication of McCoy's red-to-yellow-to-orange 1950s-style flames.

Mechanically, a lot had transpired in the hot rod in the 45 or so years between McCoy's original car build and Kinnaman's, and Dave incorporated the advantageous

new stuff. He used a Chevy 350 engine with a Corvette intake and Quadrajet carb. For long-distance travel, the Chevy mill is backed by an overdrive 200-4R transmission and an 8-inch Ford rear end. Mustang II front suspension components carried the advantage of disc front brakes. Diamondback radial tires are another nod to modern technology that really makes a difference on the highway.

Note the mega-pinstriped white firewall by Keni Hill. Stock 1940 seats were covered in red-and–white, rolled-and-pleated vinyl by Ray Brown of Muncie, Indiana. Vickie

did like this car, past tense, but it was sold to Mike Miraglia of San Leandro, California. Even top-notch car builders like Kinnaman have to sell one hot rod to finance the next one.

Ford Deluxe

Flames by:
The Rod Doctor

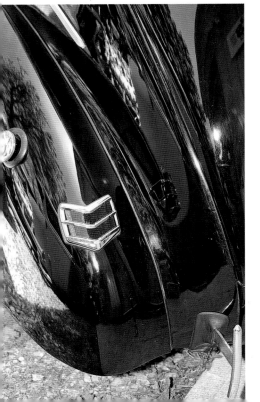

What strikes an observer first about Chris Vannarsdall's 1930 Model A pickup is the overall look. The proportions are just right, including the amount of the 3.5-inch chop and the 10.5-inch-shortened bed. If a guy goes for the extra half inch, it says that he checked and double-checked the proportions to make it look just right. Chris' truck also has a quality of build that shows it was done by someone who took care to make sure the panels line up properly, nothing is rubbing that's not supposed to, and the car is safe.

1930 FORD PICKUP

Owner: Chris Vannarsdall
Builder: Chris Vannarsdall
Engine: 1951 Chrysler Hemi
Photographer: Alan Mayes

Chris is an engineer/tool and die maker/ mold maker. People in that field build sweet hot rods because they are used to working tolerances in the 100,000ths of an inch. They don't have to be that precise in building a car, but the 64ths and 32nds are

nothing to these guys. They can eyeball that close!

Chris found the cab and frame in Chicago, and everything else was located close to home (Scottsburg, Indiana). He built the truck almost single-handedly. That includes all the chopping and 4 inches of channeling, rebuilding the '51 Chrysler Hemi, painting, and everything. He narrowed the Franklin quick-change and built his own exhaust and intake manifold.

It took Chris about three years to gather all the parts and another year and a half to build the truck. Inspiration came from older hot rodding friends and his father-in-law's original 1950s and 1960s rod magazines. That is why this truck has a timeless look.

Did You Know?
Chris Vannarsdall followed a tried and true recipe for a low-buck interior—do it yourself. He used a '36 Chevy truck dash, a homemade column topped by a Hudson steering wheel, and a seat he built out of plywood and foam. Friend Tom Collins did the upholstery.

Larry Harper hails from Hixson, Tennessee, just outside Chattanooga, and he builds hot rods for a living at his Traditional Hot Rods shop. Larry's Model A fits the name of his shop, for sure.

It's a 1930 steel body, chopped 2.5 inches and channeled 4 inches. The cowl was filled, and the Model A truck bed was shortened a just-right 8 inches. Hey, it's not going to carry much beyond a cooler and the gas tank anyway. The cab was moved back 6 inches, which allowed clearance for the engine without cutting the firewall. Two antique carpenter's levels were used as bedrails.

1930 FORD PICKUP

Owner: Larry Harper
Builder: Larry Harper
Engine: 1955 Chrysler Hemi
Photographer: Alan Mayes

Motivation for this little jewel comes from a 1955 Chrysler Hemi, a 331-cube version, bored 0.060 inch over and running an Iskenderian cam. Hot Heads provided the headers and intake. That is backed up with a 1992 Chevy-Getrag five-speed for just the right combo of patch-laying torque delivery

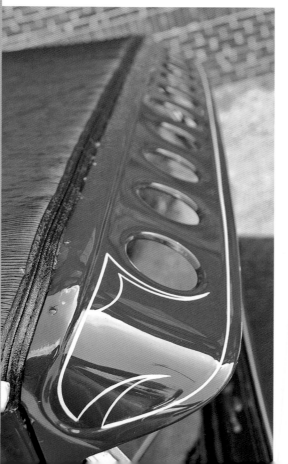

and low-rpm cruising, depending on which notch the gear shift sits in. A 9-inch Ford rear with 4.11 gears is out back.

Suspension is a mix of Pete & Jake's, Ford, and Posies. The frame was boxed back to the cab, then 2x4-inch tubing was kicked up 10 inches over the rear end. Brakes combine pretty, plated, finned Buick drums in front with Lincoln backing plates. The Ford rear end's drums were retained in back. American Torq Thrust wheels wear Firestone tires from Coker. That's traditional too, especially if you're close to Chattanooga.

Did You Know?
Traditional hot rods nearly always blend together a variety of usable, period-style components. This truck's bench seat is covered in leather, and the door panels are stock hardboard. There's also an old-time Arvin heater. A Speedway Hot Rod column mounts a Grant wood-trimmed steering wheel. Stewart-Warner gauges are mounted in a Cushman panel.

1930 FORD PICKUP

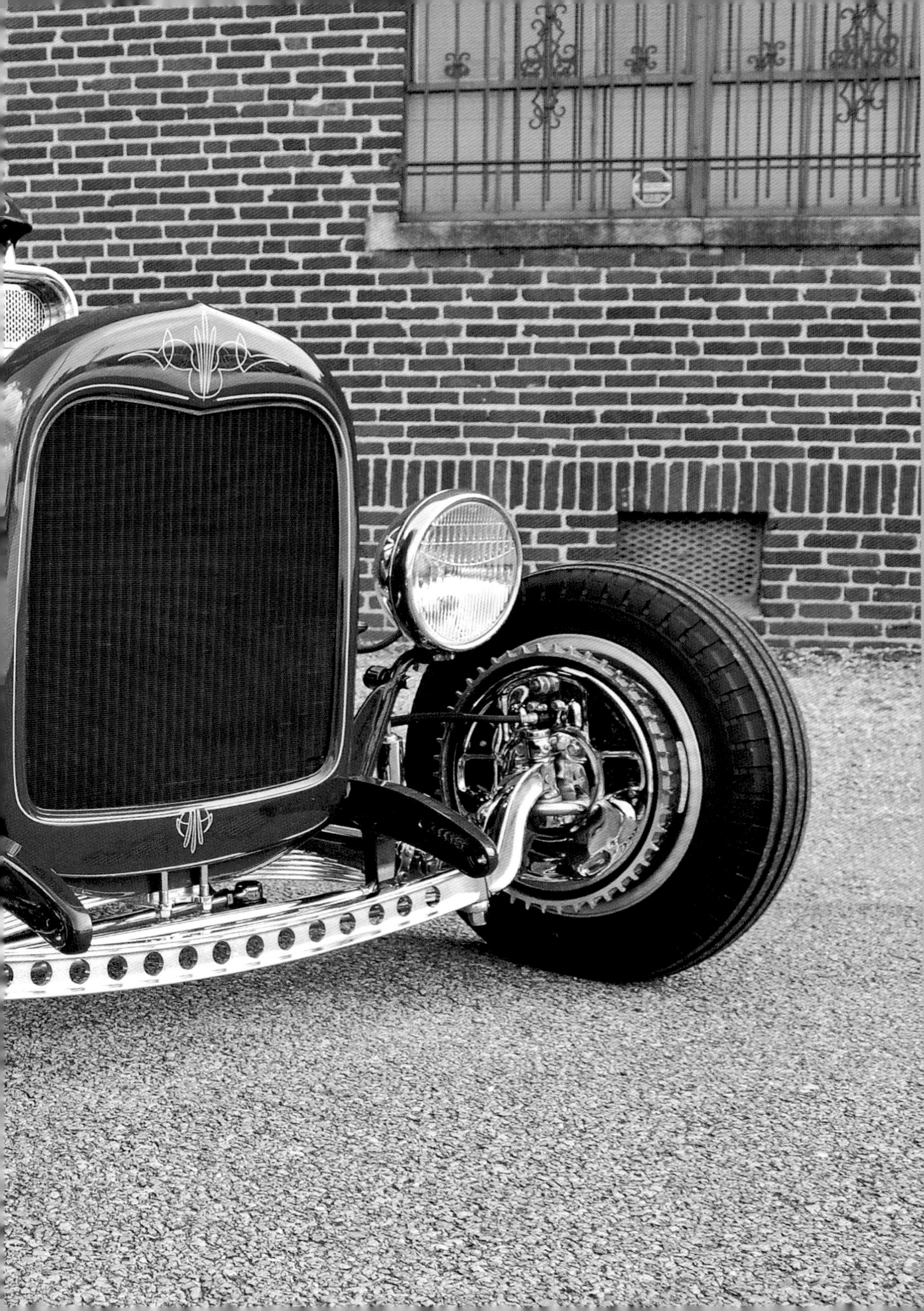

"Voodoo" is a fitting name for Voodoo Larry Grobe, since the man can most assuredly work some voodoo on a hot rod. Larry names all of his cars, and this one is tagged *Voodoo Psychosis*. It's a 1931 Ford Model A coupe on sectioned 1932 Ford frame rails.

Larry found a complete Model A on eBay, but he just wanted the body, so he took it off and sold the rest. The body had lower rust, so those areas were replaced with all-new patch panels. A brand-new deck lid and a new rear pan were also fitted. The rear panel is louvered in order to ventilate the rear-mounted radiator. The roof was chopped 6 inches.

All interior panels and seats, the heater, and the stone guard were custom made by Mike Mecurio out of Georgia. The

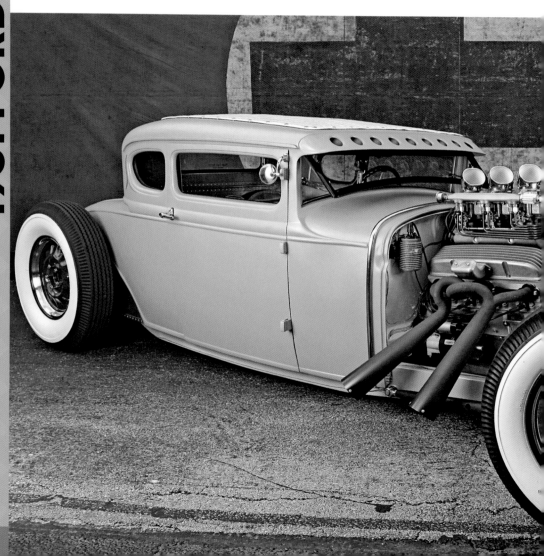

seat pads, top, and carpet were covered by upholsterer Stitch, who works out of Larry's shop (Voodoo Larry Kustoms, Schaumburg, Illinois). The paint was expertly sprayed by Hired Gun Paintwerks in St. Charles, Illinois. All that pretty pinstriping came from Voodoo Larry himself. Gus at Hot Rod Playground in Plainfield, Illinois, handled the wiring using vintage-style, cloth-wrapped wire.

Larry picked a Chevy 350 small-block with an Offenhauser six-carb cross-ram manifold to motivate the car and Holley 94 carbs to provide fuel. The transmission is a fully polished Turbo 350 feeding torque to a 1965 Chevy Posi-Traction rear end.

Alongside the drilled Magnum dropped-beam axle are matching headlight and shock mounts. Brakes are finned Buick drums with Wilson Welding's finned backing plates. The frame has a custom-made X-member and custom front and rear crossmembers. It has a 13-inch kickup in the rear with a tri-link setup and coil-over shocks. The fuel lines were custom formed by Bob at Hollywood Customs.

Those interesting headlights are vintage E&Js; taillights are courtesy of a 1937 Chrysler. Wheels are 1934 Dodge artillery-style with 6.00-16 Firestone wide whites on the front and 7.50s on the rear.

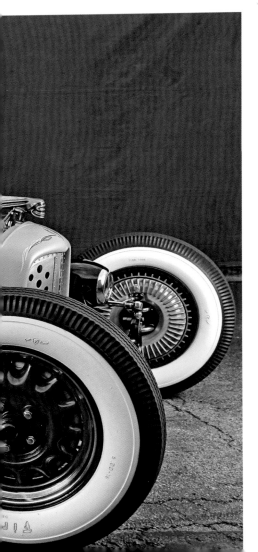

1931 FORD COUPE

Owner: Voodoo Larry Grobe
Builder: Voodoo Larry Grobe
Engine: 1980 Chevy 350
Photographer: Roy Varga

Did You Know?

Sectioning the 1932 Ford frame rails (Deuce rails are a pretty tall 6 inches) by 2 inches gives the illusion of the car being channeled, even though it isn't. That procedure also helps maintain head room inside, a big consideration for tall drivers like Voodoo Larry Grobe.

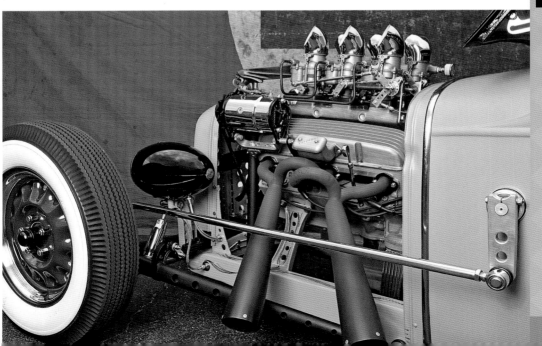

If you look at it and can't tell when it was built, *that's* a traditional hot rod. Look at Axle Idzardi's '36 Ford coupe here. This baby is spot-on perfect for what Axle was trying to accomplish: build a safe, good-looking, traditional hot rod that defies distinctions of time. The genuine "Tijuana tuck 'n' roll" interior won't give it away, nor will the owner-applied, poly primer, blue suede exterior.

Axle, a member of the Shifter Car Club, said he found the car in 2005, just before

1936 FORD COUPE
Owner: Axle Idzardi
Builder: Axle Idzardi
Engine: 1952 Ford 8BA flathead
Photographer: Mitzi Valenzuela

Christmas, and spent almost two years building it. The car had been sitting in Whittier, California, since 1962 and had some rust issues in the roof. Fabian Valdez of Vintage Hammer made some new pieces and

welded them in to replace all the damaged areas. Fabian also assisted in fabricating other pieces not currently reproduced. The louvered hood came courtesy of Eric Vaughn in Pasadena, California.

The 284-cubic-inch 8BA Ford flathead is bored, stroked, ported, polished, balanced, and relieved. It utilizes Johnson adjustable valves and an Isky cam, along with high-compression Offenhauser heads. It also has a Thickstun high-rise intake with a pair of Stromberg 97 carbs featuring Scott tops.

Ignition is via a Mallory crab-style, dual-point distributor.

The 1939 Ford transmission feeds power back to a '36 Ford rear end with 3.54 gears. Brakes are 1940 Ford hydraulics. Tires are wide whitewall Firestone bias-plies mounted on 16-inch Ford steel wheels.

Did You Know?

The chassis on this 1936 Ford is as traditional as it gets. Front suspension consists of a 4-inch-dropped Mor-Drop axle with a mono leaf spring, unsplit wishbones, and tube shocks. In the rear is a stock spring on original Houdaille shocks. The rear chassis crossmember was pie-cut and flattened.

1936 FORD COUPE

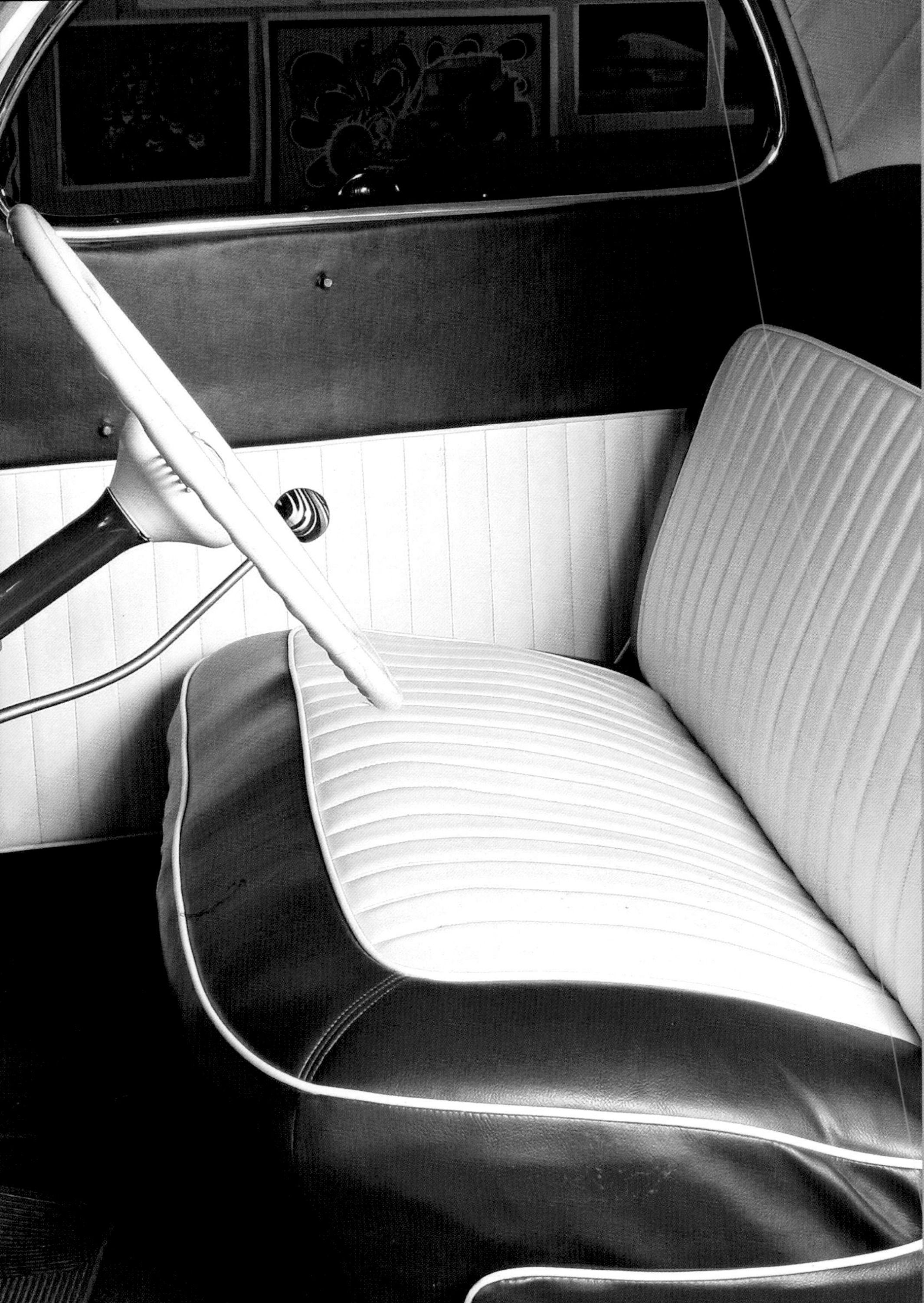

You better read this because when you look at the pictures of this car, you're definitely not seeing what you think you are. Although it looks exactly like a '27 Ford Model T roadster body on a Deuce frame, it isn't either (a T body or a Deuce frame). The body and

1927 "COSSIN FORD"

Owner: Eddie Cossin
Builder: Eddie Cossin
Engine: 1976 302 Ford
Photographer: Max Duryea

frame on this car were completely hand-built by Eddie Cossin. That's right, hand-built at his shop, Fast Eddie's Hotrods in Albuquerque, New Mexico.

The car started out as five sheets of 18-gauge steel for the body and two sheets of 10-gauge for the frame. He built everything, including the Duvall windshield, the air cleaner, and the exhaust manifolds, as well as the '32 frame and '32 grille shell, thanks to a loaner for measurements from a good friend. Yes, the dashboard is homemade too.

The engine is a stock-specification 302 Ford backed up by a C4 transmission. The only enhancements are an Edelbrock carb and a Pertronix ignition module. The front axle is a drilled and dropped Model A axle— the drilling and dropping done by Cossin, of course. The rear end is an 8.8-inch Ford.

Did You Know?
Not only did Eddie Cossin hand-build the body, frame, and Duvall-style windshield of this car, he hand-built them all on an English wheel and helve hammer that he also built himself. He built the tools and then built the car with them.

Joaquin Arnett, of the legendary San Diego Bean Bandits, built this 1934 Ford coupe hot rod in 1950 and 1951. Andy Granatelli owned it briefly, and then Bill Couch bought it at a used car lot in 1953. He's owned it ever since.

Couch saw the car in the first issue of *Honk!* magazine and had the picture hanging on his bulletin board at home. He could hardly believe his eyes when he saw it on that Chicago car lot. He was 16 years old but somehow convinced his dad to loan him the money to buy it.

1934 FORD COUPE

Owner: Bill Couch
Builder: Joaquin Arnett
Engine: 1934 Ford flathead
Photographer: Alan Mayes

During the time Granatelli had the car, he took it to his race shop in Chicago and added Grancor heads and a few other goodies. He also had the car repainted a cream color. Arnett had originally done it in black.

In 1996, Bill decided it was time to restore the old beauty to Granatelli's specs. Mark Kirby at Motor City Flathead in Dundee, Michigan, got the nod for the engine rebuild. Upholstery was handled by Scott "Willie" Pert and matches the original parchment and avocado vinyl. Bodywork was restored by Paul Reitter, who still asserts that Joaquin Arnett was a master metalworker. The paint was applied in Port Huron at Watters Works, while Greg Bock laid on the pinstripes.

Couch's '34 coupe looks from all angles like a scaled-down '34 Ford. Except for the width, all other proportions have been altered, including the 11 inches that Arnett took out of the length and 4 inches that the top was chopped.

Did You Know?

Horsepower was the name of the game for the Granatelli brothers, so when they worked over the mill for Andy's coupe, they did it in style. The engine received a bore and stroke to 276 cubic inches, a set of Grancor (Granatelli Corporation) finned aluminum heads, and a Grancor dual intake manifold.

Jason Graham, from Portland, Tennessee, is fast earning a reputation as one of the top traditional hot rod builders in the South. This red 1930 Model A sedan is a prime example of why. Jason's *modus operandi* is simple: build a cool car; take it to a Goodguys show; sell it to one of several anxious, drooling hot rod fans who know perfection when they see it; and then go home and build something else. Johnny Powell was the buyer of this one.

Graham has no qualms about going a *long* way to acquire just the right raw material for his hot rods, either. The body and doors of this one were found languishing in dry North Dakota.

Keeping the car roadworthy is a priority for Graham, so much attention goes into the brakes and running gear. The front axle is a 4-inch-dropped I-beam with a Durant mono leaf spring. Front brakes are '48 Ford drums fed by a Corvette master cylinder. The steering is a Unisteer cross-steer rack and pinion.

Pure hot rod nostalgia resides in the coolest engine that a hot rod can have: a Chevy 348 with three deuces and a hot cam. It's backed by a Wilwood hydraulic clutch and a five-speed manual transmission from a Chevy S-10.

One distinguishing feature of the car is its louvered top—348 louvers, to be exact. The top was chopped 5 inches, and the body was channeled 3 inches.

1930 FORD SEDAN

Owner: Johnny Powell
Builder: Jason Graham
Engine: 1959 Chevy 348
Photographer: Jack Criswell

Did You Know?

The frame for this rod was designed on a CAD (computer-aided-drafting) machine, including tapered front horns like the original, and then it was laser cut at a friend's shop from 2x4-inch rectangular tubing. Just like rodders of old, Graham used the latest technology to make the car as good as it can be.

In 1954, mechanic Bill Waddill of Swartz Creek, Michigan, acquired a 1932 Ford sedan from a junkyard. He immediately asked local hot rodder Red Abbey to chop the top 3¾ inches. Not 4 inches, not 3½. It was a just-right 3¾ inches. He also painted the car gray with white flames and added the car's first hot rod engine: an Olds Rocket. The car became his daily driver.

In 1958, Waddill started running National Hot Rod Association (NHRA) events and replaced the engine with a powerful Chrysler 392 Hemi. A roll bar was also installed, as was some strategically

placed concrete under the rear seat area to help with traction.

At the 1958 NHRA National Drags in Tulsa, the car won the B/G title. By 1966 the car was in the possession of John Spatrisano, who installed a built 389 out of a 1963 Pontiac that had been rolled. That engine was the impetus for the car's current appearance.

In 1971 the car passed to Jim Lischkge, who pulled the Pontiac and installed a 327 Chevy. He owned it until 1979, when it passed to current owner, Dennis Lesky. Dennis had seen the car previously and had tried to buy the dashboard out of it for the Stewart-Warner instrument panel and 1958 NHRA Nationals decal.

These days, this survivor car resides in Ionia, Michigan, and is the calling card for Lesky's Ionia Hot Rod Shop. It is now powered by a 350 Chevy engine out of a dump truck and a Turbo 350 automatic.

The Ford has the original seats and the original chicken-wire–supported fabric top insert. The '40 Ford steering wheel is mounted on a homemade column. Brakes are 1946 Ford units in Buick finned drums.

1932 FORD SEDAN
Owner: Dennis Lesky
Builder: Bill Waddill
Engine: 1970 Chevy 350
Photographer: Alan Mayes

Did You Know?
This 1932 Ford was named *Regret* in 1966 by a former owner who drag raced the car. His regret was that he had $7,000 in 1966 dollars tied up in its Stover and Company-built 389 Pontiac race engine! That's also when the hood lettering was added.

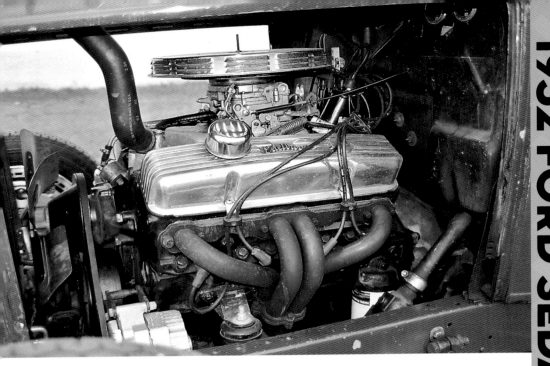

PARTICIPANT 1958
4th ANNUAL
NATIONAL CHAMPIONSHIP
DRAG RACES
OKLAHOMA CITY · OKLAHOMA
Courtesy of
MOON EQUIPMENT CO.

MEETS
SEMA
SPECS

When this beautifully crafted roadster shows up at a rod run, folks scratch their heads, confer with buddies, and then finally ask, "What is it?" The confusion is understandable because although the car has some familiar-looking componentry (like the sectioned original '32 Ford grille shell and the inverted '49 Hudson taillights), the body is obviously not the ubiquitous Ford, and the unusual dashboard offers few clues.

1927 ESSEX ROADSTER

Owner: Sam Hornish Jr.
Builder: Gary Brown
Engine: 1977 Chevy 355 small-block
Photographer: Alan Mayes

The body on this car is a 1927 Essex roadster and features hand-built doors that open and shut like those on a new car.

Gary Brown of Brown's Metal Mods in Indianapolis, Indiana, built the car. The body is channeled over the frame, but the floorpan is *under* the frame, which gives an additional 4 inches of interior height and leg room. That dashboard is a combination of the Essex lower and a custom fabricated upper, housing a 1958 Edsel instrument cluster. Upholstery was done by Dave Martinez.

Powering this beauty is a 355 Chevy small-block with Patriot aluminum heads. The engine is topped off by an Edelbrock Air-Gap dual quad setup and Corvette air cleaners. The tranny is a manual-bodied, built Turbo 350, and the exhaust runs through modified Speedway Motors fenderwell headers tied to custom baffled pipes.

Did You Know?

The top on this car, currently owned by race car driver Sam Hornish Jr., is hand-built from canvas and epoxy and is translucent. Builder Gary Brown made the Duvall-style windshield and the doors. The rear bumper was made from two aluminum baseball bats that were welded together and polished.

INDIANA
97 X 1970
www.IN.gov

Chadly Johnson knew exactly what he wanted when he set out to build this 1930 Ford Model A hot rod.

"My goal was to build a hot rod that has the appearance of a barn find," he says, "something I found, tuned up, put fresh gas and a battery in, and started driving."

He certainly succeeded on two fronts. He got the look he was after, and he drives it, a lot. The Eau Claire, Wisconsin, engineering technician has put several thousand miles on the car since he finished its three-year-long build, a build that included chopping the top on the pretty nice coupe by 7½ inches. A 1932 Ford grille shell sits out front. The car still wears its original black paint,

which has held up pretty darned well. Inside, there's a stock dashboard, a steering column made of an exhaust tube, and a Mexican blanket for a seat cover.

Mechanically, Chadly's coupe is textbook traditional hot rod if anyone's is. He pulled a Chrysler 331 Hemi from a low-mileage

Did You Know?

Befitting the torque from the Hemi, Chadly Johnson used a Ford 9-inch rear end located by a four-link suspension on his coupe. In front is a Super Bell dropped I-beam axle with disc brakes on a transverse leaf spring.

1954 four-door New Yorker. Behind that is a Muncie four-speed transmission. A Weiand Drag Star intake carries six Ford/Holley carbs. The stock Chrysler ignition still works fine. Open lake headers are by Gear Drive. Firestone bias-ply blackwalls on 16-inch steel wheels fit the theme of the car perfectly.

1930 FORD COUPE

Owner: Chadly Johnson
Builder: Chadly Johnson
Engine: 1954 Chrysler 331 Hemi
Photographer: Chadly Johnson

Bob Merkt Jr.'s 1932 Ford roadster has been in the family since 1956, passing through the hands of several family members but never leaving the Merkt family. Purchased by Bob's grandfather, the original package consisted of a '32 frame, some unknown cowl, and the back half of a '29 Ford coupe. Bob's uncle Miles Merkt adapted a 1932 Fordor sedan cowl and doors. With his dad's help, Miles assembled the car, channeling the body over a Z'ed frame. Miles lost interest, and it passed to his brother, Bob Sr., who installed an Oldsmobile engine with six carburetors in 1962. In 1968, Bob Sr. dropped in a 283 Chevy engine with a three-speed.

The 283 didn't have enough power, so in went a big-block 396. The extra weight of the big block was too much, and the car lost its feel of balance. In went a 365-horsepower 327 out of a Corvette, which was just right. Bob Sr. lost interest in the car after a while too, and it sat for several years, until it was finally passed to Bob Jr.

Bob took everything down to bare metal, replaced the floor, and patched places in the body. He lowered the car a couple of inches, chopped the windshield, and fashioned a new front spreader/nerf bar.

A 1949 Mercury dashboard was sectioned to fit. Chris Theames in Madison, Wisconsin, stitched the tuck-and-roll vinyl interior in a 1950s period-correct design.

Bob dropped in a built 301 Chevy small-block engine. He retained the custom-built

Did You Know?

In the late 1950s and early 1960s, this '32 Ford roadster was well-known around the Milwaukee area. Teen heartthrobs, the Crescendos, visited to do a local TV show and performed a song in the car during the show. Their hit song, which sold a million copies, was "Oh, Julie," which was released in 1957.

headers that Russ Sacs had made 40 years before. The car has a four-speed manual transmission.

The roadster has appeared in a few magazines over the years and was featured in the DVD *Mad Fabricators Society Volume One*.

1932 FORD ROADSTER

Owner: Bob Merkt Jr.
Builder: The Merkt Family
Engine: 1969 Chevy 301 small-block
Photographer: Alan Mayes

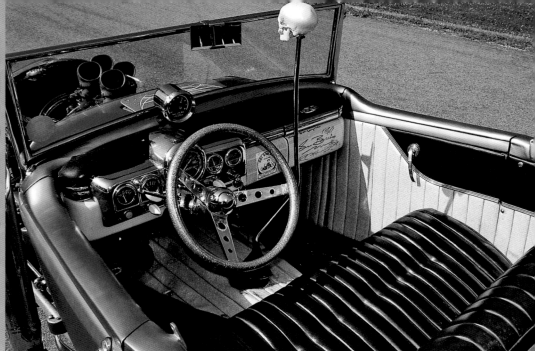

This 1939 Ford Deluxe Tudor belongs to Mike Goodman, president of the world-famous Honest Charley Speed Shop in Chattanooga. A hot rodder for most of his adult life, he actually worked several years at the original Honest Charley shop with "Honest Hisself." His '39 is a bit of a rolling advertisement for the speed shop, since it is a traditional hot rod, Honest's specialty, and it is equipped with quite a few goodies from the Honest Charley inventory of parts,

1939 FORD SEDAN

Owner: Mike Goodman
Builder: Joe Smith
Engine: 1949 Ford truck flathead
Photographer: Alan Mayes

along with some vintage pieces. It was built by Joe Smith of Joe Smith Early Ford in Marietta, Georgia, a well-known rod builder in the Southeast.

Induction on the 1949 Ford truck flathead engine is handled by the Stromberg 97 carburetors on an Edelbrock manifold. Ported and relieved Navarro heads cover Ross pistons and Chevy six-cylinder valves actuated by an Isky 1007 cam. The engine was built by Bradley Dennis and Joe Smith.

The suspension wears the most modern parts. Posies springs are used at both ends, as are Chassis Engineering sway bars. A Super Bell 4-inch-dropped front axle and spindles connect to Pete & Jake's shocks and disc brakes. Steering is through a stock '39 column with Vega cross steering, and Mike hangs on to a banjo wheel while he's steering this baby. The rear end is a coveted Halibrand quick-change center with 9-inch Ford axles.

This car is a very good example of a traditional sedan hot rod. It's simple, tasteful, and quick.

Did You Know?

Almost everyone in the old car hobby will say his or her favorite fat-fendered Ford is the 1940. Hardly anyone will mention the '39, yet the two have the same silhouette. Most body panels are interchangeable. The '39 Deluxe and '40 Standard grilles are nearly identical to each other.

Is this the perfect Deuce coupe hot rod? If not, it comes very, very close. Neal East is the owner, but he'll be the first to tell you that all the credit for it goes to Don Coleman. Former editor of *Rod & Custom* magazine, Neal knows hot rods and has built a few himself. He lives in Littleton, Colorado.

1932 FORD COUPE

Owner: Neal East
Builder: Don Coleman
Engine: 1948 Mercury flathead
Photographer: Alan Mayes

Don Coleman found this car's body in the woods and built on that foundation. He did it all—chassis, brakes, paint, upholstery, top chop, and everything.

Check the reflections in the black paint on this ebony jewel. It takes a very smooth body to wear black paint successfully. The top is chopped 3 inches, a number that is just about right in most cases.

Neal's '32 is powered by a 1948 Mercury flathead. It blows out through headers and dual Smithy's mufflers. The Edelbrock heads match an Edelbrock intake manifold and connect to Stromberg 97s. The transmission is a traditional '39 Ford gearbox.

Front brakes from a Ford F-150 pickup are mounted inside Buick finned aluminum brake drums. The rear end comes from a 1936 Ford.

Black-and-white tuck-and-roll upholstery covers the original '32 bench seat. Coleman did the interior himself. A 1956 Ford truck donated its steering column, which mounts a '39 Ford banjo steering wheel. The dashboard is a filled '32 panel with eight Stewart-Warner gauges.

A very rare and unusual Colorado Lost license plate with the number 1932 is actually registered to this car. What are the chances?

Did You Know?

The Coleman nameplate mounted on Neal East's coupe is from a Denver-built Coleman truck. Coleman built heavy-duty trucks, airport tractors, and four-wheel-drive conversions for many decades. Neal leaves the nameplate on there to pay homage to the gent who built his beautiful coupe.

1932 FORD COUPE

LOST 1932
COLORADO 1932

Coleman

Roy Caruthers' '31 Ford roadster was built in the style of early "dual purpose" hot rods: weekend racers and daily drivers. Roy, a former racer from a family of racers around the Indianapolis area, was born in the era of backyard-built sprint cars and midgets.

The '31 has some Indy-based racing connections in its componentry. The Winters quick-change rear end center section is from the last midget race car that Roy owned. Andy Hurtebise, son of the late Indy 500

1931 FORD ROADSTER

Owner: Roy Caruthers
Builder: Roy Caruthers
Engine: 1949 Ford flathead
Photographer: Alan Mayes

driver, Jim Hurtebise, helped Roy with the machine work to get the quick-change sprint car hubs and real knock-offs to mate to 8-inch Ford axles and '40 Ford axle housings.

The dash center section from a 1953 DeSoto resides on a dashboard that Roy Caruthers and his friend, Tom Culbertson, formed over an oxygen bottle. The taillights were pulled from an unidentified Chrysler.

Denny Jamison, who owns Hammer Art Automotive in Indianapolis, helped with the louvered hood and applied the black paint to the car. The numbers and lettering came from Dan Shaw.

Power for the *C&C Special* is courtesy of a 1949 Ford flattie. The engine wears an original vintage Offenhauser manifold and three Stromberg 97 carburetors. Ignition is Mallory, and headers are homemade. A Schneider cam and Ross pistons round out the speed equipment list. The five-speed transmission and cut-down seat are both out of an S-10 pickup. Front wheels are vintage 16-inch Halibrands carrying 6.00 tires, while the rear Halibrands wear 7.00x18 tires.

Did You Know?
The rear 18-inch Halibrand Indy car wheels were actually on A. J. Foyt's 1962 Indianapolis 500 car. The left one fell off his car right after a pit stop and very possibly cost him the race win. Roy traded a weed eater for that wheel! That's swapping at its finest.

1931 FORD ROADSTER

1931 FORD ROADSTER

This 1933 Ford pickup was a hot rod when Josh Mills got it. It had a reasonable 3½-inch top chop but had been overly channeled, so Josh and Hank Young "unchanneled" it a bit. The cab was also moved back about 4 inches. There was considerable rust in the truck's panels, so Josh and Hank replaced a few inches worth all the way around and modified the firewall a bit for their engine of choice.

With the cab work done, the truck's bed looked too long, so 9½ inches were removed. Six rows of six louvers perforate the tailgate.

1933 FORD PICKUP

Owner: Josh Mills
Builder: Josh Mills
Engine: 1959 Buick 401 Nailhead
Photographer: Alan Mayes

A 1932 Ford truck grille shell completes the look.

Josh rebuilt a '59 Buick 401 Nailhead engine for his truck, boring it out to 409 cubes. An Offenhauser manifold/Holley carb tri-power setup is used, along with

a Schneider camshaft. A Ronco magneto supplies the spark. An M22 four-speed sits behind the Nailhead.

A 9-inch rear end out of a 1957 Ford is attached to a custom crossmember via a '37 Ford trailing arm. The front axle is a drilled and dropped I-beam located by '46 split wishbones.

Genuine B-17 bomber seats were acquired from an Alabama airplane graveyard, and Josh stitched black rolled-and-pleated covers. Aviation seatbelts complete the look. The '33 Ford dashboard has 1950s Stewart-Warner black-faced gauges. The steering wheel is from a 1940 Ford. The steering box and shifter both came from a '39 Ford. The tachometer mounted under the dash is an actual Westach from 1951. Door handles and window cranks were once in a 1950 Ford.

Did You Know?

Josh Mills' 1933 Ford truck is an excellent example of some of the newer-built hot rods that defy the casual observer's attempts to date the build. This truck could have been built in 1959, 1964, or 2002. It's a timeless style, and it uses timeless components.

Scott Karuza started his search for a hot rod at "old man Stoke's ranch" on the other side of Santa Rosa, California. Retired carpenter Fred Stoke builds flat-black, 1933–1934, full-fendered Ford pickup trucks with 2-inch chops. That's all he builds. No other chop and no other color. So Scott bought one of them and then proceeded to modify it to suit his own taste.

Scott is a self-employed plumber, and his employees are hot rodders, so when they're not laying pipe, they use the shop to work on their cars. Scott's truck became a company project and calling card. He and his employees, Rory Allen and Tom Riehl, named the project *Koppertone* and modeled it as a show truck that could have been touring in the middle of the twentieth century.

The top of this hot rod was chopped 3½ inches more than Fred Stoke's original mini-chop. The truck's bed was shortened 10 inches. Period-style nerf bars were fabricated by Paul Shaughnessy of New Metal Kustoms to replace the stock bumpers. The upholstery and angel-hair headliner were done by Chris Plante of Ace High Upholstery.

For the chassis, a Magnum 5-inch-dropped axle was drilled and chromed and then hung off a Posies 2-inch-drop chrome spring. So Cal Speed Shop hairpins and bat wings keep everything located properly. Custom '39 Ford, polished, cast-aluminum, finned backing plates from Wilson Machine in Texas are paired with '59 Buick polished aluminum drums. B. F. Goodrich whitewall tires are in front. Radir pie-cut whitewall slicks bring up the rear in true hot rod style.

1934 FORD PICKUP

Owner: Scott Karuza
Builder: Fred Stoke/Scott Karuza
Engine: 1966 Chevy 327
Photographer: Mitzi Valenzuela

Did You Know?

This truck is powered by a 327 Chevy bored 0.040 inch over. An Edelbrock and Rochester tri-power provide fuel. Reworked heads and a rare 30-30 Duntov cam add power. The transmission is a '62 Corvette Super T-10 four-speed.

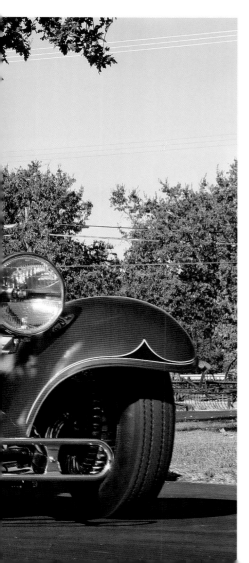

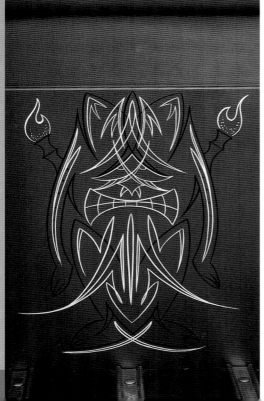

In 1955, Michigan native Bill Couch was a freshman at the University of Arizona. He bought this '32 roadster during that first year of school. Freshmen were not allowed to keep cars on campus, so Bill kept the roadster in a rented garage a mile away from campus. It was there that he transformed the '32 Ford roadster into the hot rod he has owned for over 55 years.

When the transformation was complete, the roadster sported a 1948 Ford flathead backed up with a '39 gearbox. Well-known sprint car fabricator, driver, and Hall of Famer Granvel "Hank" Henry created the dropped tube axle and matching wishbones.

In 1957, Bill shipped the roadster back home to Michigan, along with spare parts. The movers "lost" the hood for the car. The

pink hood that now appears on the car was a spare that Bill had picked up at a swap meet in Arizona.

While Bill went back to school, his brother took the '32 drag racing. He gutted the body to make it lighter and removed many of the braces. The roadster was later stripped of race parts and spent the next 40 years being moved from one barn to another on the family farm. However, Bill has passed on the gearhead gene to his two sons, Billy and John. Having grown up with Dad's roadster as a permanent family fixture, these gents were eager to resurrect the ol' family heirloom.

John rebuilt and adjusted the original mechanical brakes so they work like they were intended. The faded pink hood has such an interesting story that it was left untouched. In addition to the movers' markings, it also has the layout lines for the louvers on the inside. One extremely rare piece on the car is the working Pine's winter grille. Its louvers can be closed, allowing the car to run warmer in cold Michigan winters.

1932 FORD ROADSTER

Owner: Bill Couch
Builder: The Couch Family
Engine: 1948 Ford flathead
Photographer: Alan Mayes

Did You Know?

The interior in Bill Couch's car is as basic as it gets. In other words: hot rod style. The driver's seat is a surplus aluminum seat from a P-51D World War II fighter airplane that Bill picked up at Davis-Monthan Air Force Base in Tucson, Arizona, around 1956. He paid $3 for it.

Once the Model T was replaced in 1928 by the Model A, it didn't take long for speed equipment makers to latch onto the new engine and start providing go-fast pieces for it. Even for several years after the flathead V-8 appeared, some potent Model A fours still ruled the roads. The 1932 Ford Model B four-cylinder was very similar to the Model A's engine and benefited from the "research" done on the Model A.

Darrel Helms and his father, Duane, learned about an early roadster hot rod stored in their area. After several years of tracking it down, they finally found and purchased it in 2002.

Having been a race car for 11 years early in its life, and then in storage for 46 years, the roadster doesn't have many miles on it, so it's in pretty good shape and even has what appears to be the original 1930 Ford paint on much of its body. It has obviously been stored inside throughout most or all of its 80 years of life.

The 1932 Model B engine has a Cook Cyclone four-port, overhead-valve head on it, along with a homemade twin-carburetor

intake manifold and Stromberg 97 carbs. Ignition is via an American Bosch side-drive magneto. There's a Winfield camshaft and a lightened flywheel.

The four-cylinder engine isn't a huge powerhouse, so the 1930 rear end is adequate to handle the souped-up power output. The transmission is a 1932 case with 1939 gears. The front end is a 1932 Ford commercial axle with a reversed main spring leaf. There are 1940 Ford brakes and, as a leftover testament to its dry lakes days, tow-bar mounts on the backing plates.

1930 FORD ROADSTER

Owners: Darrel and Duane Helms
Builders: Bob Hayes
Engine: 1932 Model B
Photographer: Alan Mayes

Did You Know?

This 1930 Model A roadster was originally built as a racer by Bob Hayes in 1937. Hayes' mother bought the car new in 1930! Hayes' partner, Wes Cooper, reportedly built the engine for the car, and they campaigned it on the dry lakes courses until about 1948.

COLORADO 1930
5·06·12

COOK 4·PORT A·ROAD 68
W. COOPER · B. HAYES
AN ELEC. TIMED 1·4 8:37 SEC OR 107:52 M.P.H.
COURSE MUROC DATE 9·28·41

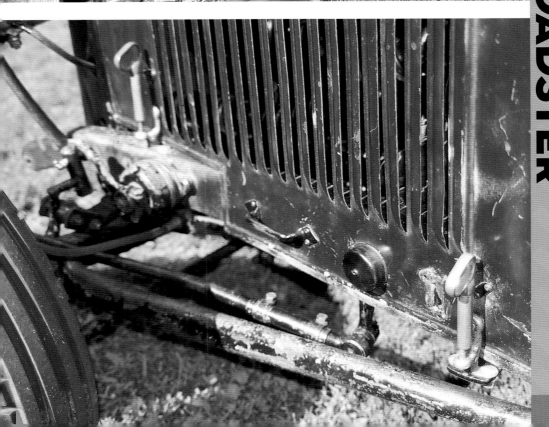

Close examination of Bill Roark's Studebaker-powered Track-T reveals that Bill is a very talented man, indeed. Bill did much of the work himself, and it rivals anything done by a professional builder. This car is rolling proof that you can build something out of the ordinary and have it look absolutely great.

There are many Track-Ts out there, and they make for a sharp and often relatively low-budget rod, but there aren't many differences among them. They're pretty simple, with a minimum of components, so what can you do?

Faced with this very dilemma, Bill Roark decided he wanted to build his Track-T in the style of the early 1950s, what he calls 1954 B.C. (before Chevy). The Chevy small-block came out in 1955 models, so Bill decided on Studebaker power (Studebaker introduced an OHV V-8 in 1951). He couldn't locate a three deuces manifold for the Stude, so he

ported the heads and adapted an Edelbrock manifold from a '49 Cadillac. No one makes sprint-car-style headers for a Studebaker engine, so Bill had to make those too.

The transmission in Bill's T is a '58 Studebaker automatic, manufactured by Borg-Warner. The rear differential is a '68 Ford 9-inch, narrowed 8½ inches, and axles are by Moser.

The headlights are J. C. Whitney specials, and they rest on perches made from the legs of an office chair! The car's '27 body and track nose are from Speedway, but Bill built the grille himself. He also built the wood-backed fiberglass dash.

1927 FORD TRACK ROADSTER

Owner: Bill Roark
Builder: Bill Roark
Engine: 1951 Studebaker V-8
Photographer: Alan Mayes

Did You Know?

The front brakes are a combination of '40 Ford backing plates and shoes in finned '63 Buick Riviera drums. They look good and stop the same way. The old-timey wire wheels are actually modern 15-inch Wheels Vintiques models. They look right, don't they?

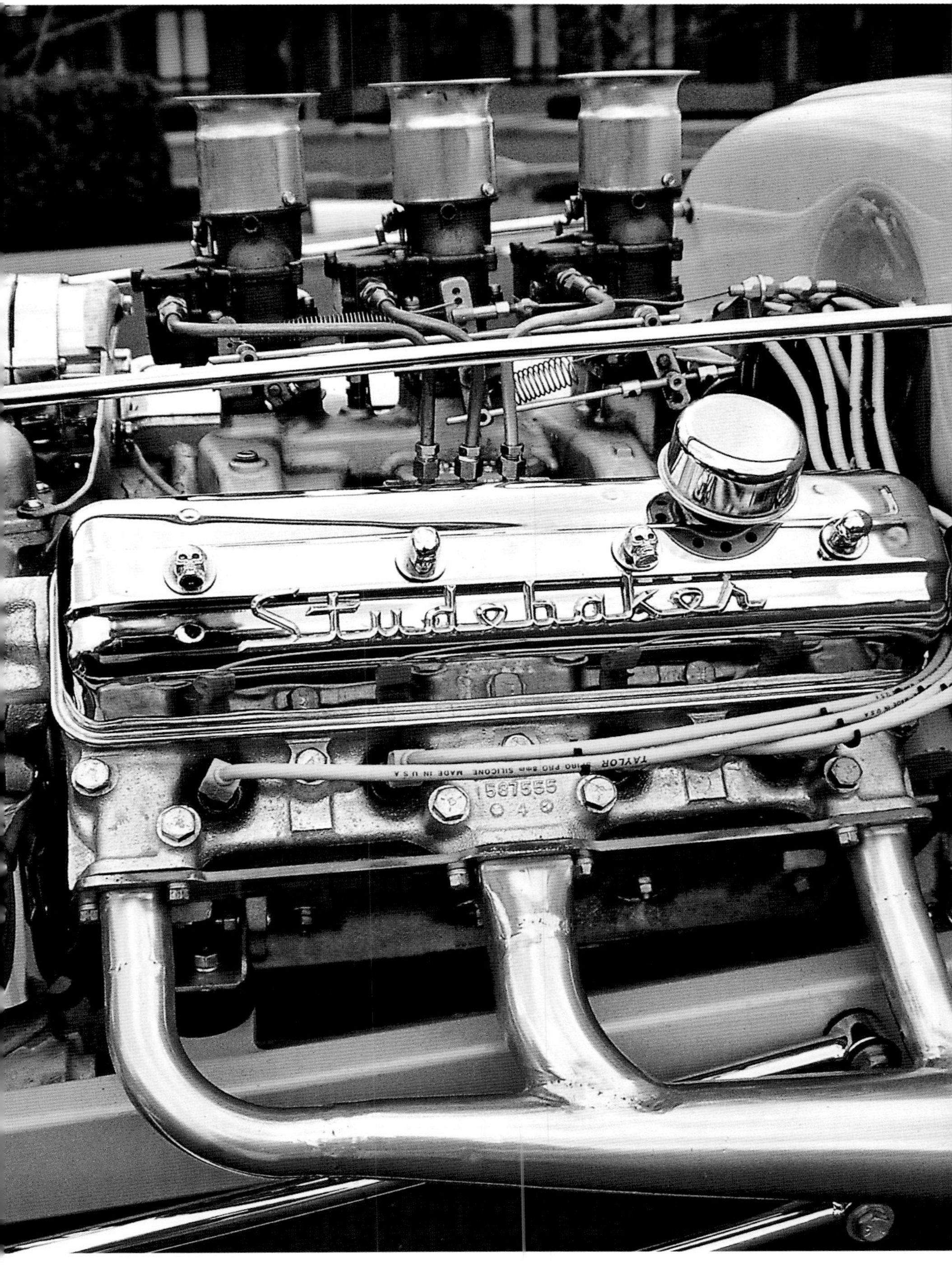
Studebaker
TAYLOR SILICONE MADE IN U S A
1587555

This 1932 Ford roadster has been a hot rod since 1948. In that first form, it was channeled and fenderless, and it sported a track nose and full hood. It was powered then by a Ford flathead and had an Auburn dash and flames.

1932 FORD ROADSTER

Owner: Greg McComas
Restoration: Rocky Mountain Street Rods
Engine: 1955 Chevy 265 V-8
Photographer: John Jackson

Throughout its several iterations since 1948, it has always been in the hands of hot rodders. Current owner Greg McComas actually found the car in 2003 through a strange series of events that revolved around the track nose being for sale on eBay (the whole story is in issue 31 of *Ol' Skool Rodz* magazine). McComas wound up with the nose and then the car. He had the car restored by Rocky Mountain Street Rods in Arvada, Colorado, where Gary Vahling led its reconstruction and helped chase its history.

Restored to its 1961 configuration, the car has a 1955 Chevy 265-cube V-8 running 1958 Corvette heads and a Weiand four-carb intake with Stromberg carburetors, backed by a 1939 Ford transmission. Jim Green Racing, of *Green Monster* fame, built the engine back then.

Additional features include: bobbed front and rear fenders, nerf bars, a chrome roll bar, and a 17-inch Bell steering wheel. Bob Ellis originally painted the hot rod 1959 Buick Lido Lavender. That was duplicated by Rocky Mountain Street Rods.

The car has an Auburn dashboard with Stewart-Warner curved glass gauges and a Sun tachometer. Jay Schluter at Pjays Upholstery in Denver duplicated the original white tuck-and-roll interior by Acme Upholstery of Seattle.

Did You Know?

Rocky Mountain Street Rods restored this 1932 Ford roadster to its 1961 configuration, as owned by Keith Treece in the height of its glory and as it appeared in the February 1961 issue of *Hot Rod* magazine. Most of the roadster's original parts were rebuilt, refinished, rechromed, and reused for the restoration.

For some reason, Willys coupes from 1940 through 1941 have become almost synonymous with the term "gasser" over the years. To be sure, there were some well-known and successful A/GS Willys coupes campaigned over the years, especially in the 1960s. Many of those have been retired and placed into museums and private collections.

There is a huge contingent of "nostalgia gassers" running these days, though. The

1940 WILLYS COUPE

Owner: Jim Wilkens
Builder: Wilkens/Smith/Conrad/Waugh
Engine: 1970 Chevy small-block
Photographer: David W. Miller

Midwest, especially around Indiana and Ohio, is a hotbed for such activity. Here's the car of one of the guys deeply involved in those events.

The Handshaker is a '40 Willys coupe owned and driven by Jim Wilkens of Brookville, Indiana. Though many Willys gassers run with a fiberglass nose, this one is all steel.

Jim, a paint and body man, started buying pieces of Willys cars in 1996. The body shell came from an old gasser in North Carolina, and other parts came out of barns at various locations. "Like a Johnny Cash car, 'One Piece at a Time,'" Jim says.

The coupe runs a 406-cubic-inch, small-block Chevy engine, based on a 1970 block and topped with a single 750 Holley carb. A four-speed Jerico transmission sends power to a Ford 9-inch rear end with 5.38 gears. Chassis work was accomplished by Mark Smith. Dale Conrad did the metal fabrication. "Big Al" Waugh turned the wrenches.

The 568-horsepower Willys made a best run of 10.70 at 128 miles per hour. It has beaten cars considered more powerful and with more exotic engines.

"I love being the little guy with one carb, four on the floor, and all the horsepower," says Jim.

Did You Know?

Jim Wilkens has successfully campaigned The Handshaker at various nostalgia racing events around the Midwest and East. He's been a class winner at the NHRA Hot Rod Reunion in Bowling Green, Kentucky; at the Gasser Reunion in Thompson, Ohio; and at the Willys Home Run in Buffalo, New York.

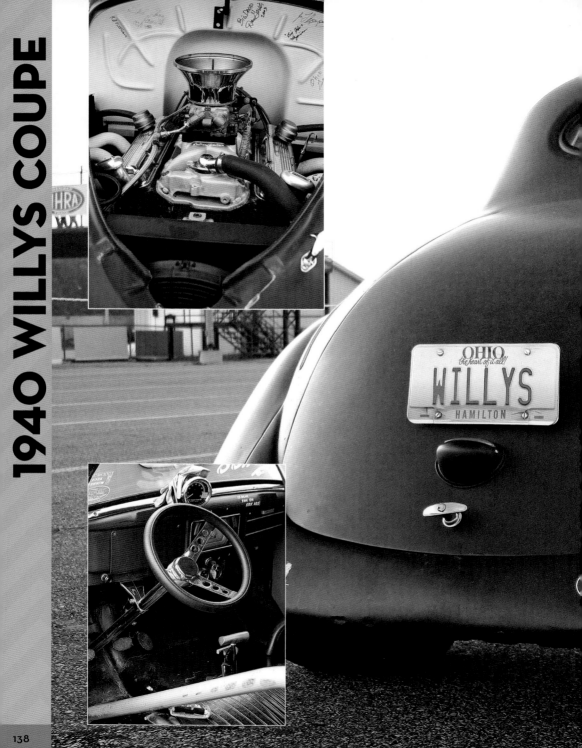

Although this Model A hot rod was built by Mark Richardson in Marietta, Georgia, it now belongs to a Frenchman, Charlie Lecach. Editor of *Kustom Garage Magazine* and *Freeway Magazines*, Charlie knows vintage iron.

"I've had a bunch of old Harleys, Indians, and vintage cars over the past 25 years, but a hot rod has always been on the wish list," Charlie says.

He sent out e-mails to friends around the globe and found Mark's 1931 Ford through a mutual friend, Josh Mills. The car had a rebuilt 1965 Mustang 289 and C4 automatic transmission and was built in a style that would allow Charlie to revise it to his own taste without undoing a lot of another guy's work.

The car was in great shape and ready to drive to Charlie's heart's content, but he

made some changes on the appearance. Mark had flames on the car, which Charlie didn't want, so now the car is just flat black. On a trip to the United States, Charlie took the 1940 Ford glovebox door and had George Sedlak pinstripe it. Sedlak painted Evel Knievel's jump bikes.

"I use this car almost daily to drive downtown to pick up my daughter at school," he says, "but also to do the weekly shopping at the supermarket or to go to meetings around France. I already crossed the country on the highway during the night, under a heavy rain without any windshield wipers."

The car has proven to be all that Charlie hoped it would be: distinctive, safe, and dependable.

1931 FORD COUPE
Owner: Charlie Lecach
Builder: Mark Richardson
Engine: 1965 Mustang 289
Photographer: Jean-Sylvain Marchessou and Eric Corlay

Did You Know?
The interior was mostly solid black when he bought the car, so Charlie Lecach transformed it with a collage of Elvgren pinups on the door panels. Red vinyl on other panels and red fur on the headliner truly transformed the interior. A red metalflake Moon steering wheel finished the job.

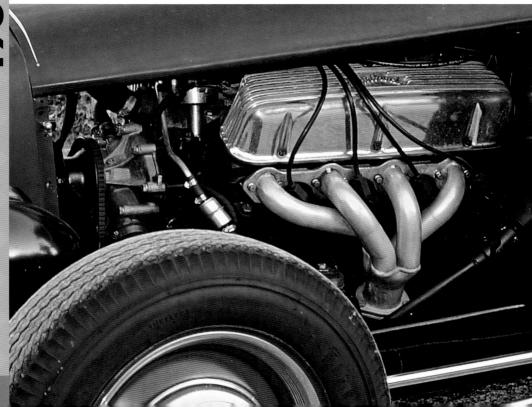

CHAPTER 2

SHOW RODS AND SPECIALS

Ah, show rods. What gearhead among us does not have memories of attending a World of Wheels, Autorama, Motorama, or Cavalcade of Customs as a child, staring longingly at the wild creations on the other side of those velvet ropes? Show rods were the mainstays and the drawing power to those indoor car shows, often held in colder climes in the winter. They also sold millions of model kits for companies like Monogram and Revell.

Far-out paint schemes; unfathomable driving positions; crushed-velvet, diamond-tuck, overstuffed seats; tires wider than those on any drivable street vehicle; and chrome, chrome, and more chrome. Rolling fantasies, that's what show rods were. They still are. Show rods are the result of artistic inspiration. Ironically, they also serve as artistic inspiration for others.

Fritz Schenck, who is responsible for two of the cars in this chapter, says that he was inspired to build show rods by two of the giants of the field, Ed "Big Daddy" Roth and Darryl Starbird. Seeing their creations when he was young encouraged him to follow in their footsteps, and since then he has become great friends with Starbird. This chapter features a clone of one of Roth's cars, *Outlaw*, built by Fritz, as well as another Roth creation, *Mega Cycle*, that he restored.

As another builder inspired by show rods, Indianapolis native Tom Culbertson was impressed by the creations of the late 1950s and early 1960s like George Barris' *Ala Kart*. So he built a car of that style, *El Tiki*, which is now owned by John and Suzie Cooper. Culbertson and the Indianapolis Road Rockets car club also run the Motorama 1962, the throwback section of the Indianapolis World of Wheels. See, inspiration.

There's a car in this chapter that is a special, one-off car. It was built over a period of two years, from 1949 to 1951, by a craftsman in the very truest sense of that word. Called the *Skylane Motor Special*, it appeared on the cover of the June 1951 issue of *Motor Trend* magazine. Built by Leroy J. Viersen Jr., with assistance from his son, Leroy III, the car features a hand-formed metal body. It wasn't hand-formed on an English wheel with a planishing hammer, either. It was hand-formed on a concrete floor using hammers and sandbags. It was built over a 1932 Ford frame, yet it looks like it could have been built by a prestigious Italian coachmaker. Carozzeria Pininfarina or Bertone would have proudly claimed it as one of their

own. It has remained in the same family since it was built and still wears its original early 1950s flathead speed equipment.

The *Skylane Motor Special* was photographed for that 1951 *Motor Trend* article and cover by well-known and highly regarded Petersen Publishing Company photographer Eric Rickman at the Verdugo Hills Golf Course in Tujunga, California. The photographs of that car in this book were taken at the same location almost 60 years later.

This chapter is a bit of a catch-all overflow for worthy cars that didn't fit the traditional hot rod or rat rod categories. The fifth car in this chapter is not a show rod or a one-off special, but it is very special nonetheless. It's more like a custom rod. It is one of the most famous cars ever built by one of the most famous custom builders of all time. Originally built in the early 1950s by young Bill Hines for an equally young Marty Ribits, the *Golden Nugget* is likely the most beautiful 1934 Ford custom hot rod ever built.

Exceptionally talented Larry Jordon fell in love with the car the first time he ever saw it. Decades later, he became its owner, lovingly and perfectly restoring it to even better condition than when it was first built. Octogenarian Bill Hines says so, and he should know.

So that's this special chapter—three show rods, a one-off, and a historic, resurrected custom rod. Five remarkable cars built by five extraordinary builders; two of them restored to better than new for more generations of car lovers to enjoy.

Tom Culbertson of Culbertson's Rods & Customs in Indianapolis has always been a car guy, and he was greatly influenced by the famous show rods of the past, such as George Barris' *Ala Kart* and Ed Roth's *Beatnik Bandit*. So he decided to build one for himself. The result is *El Tiki*, the car you see here. At least this is the final result. Owner John Cooper has embellished the car a bit, with Tom's assistance, since he acquired it.

1929 FORD ROADSTER *EL TIKI*

Owner: John Cooper
Builder: Tom Culbertson
Engine: 1955 Oldsmobile 324 V-8
Photographer: Craig Mayes

Based on a Culbertson tube frame and a reworked 1929 Ford Model A Sport Coupe body, *El Tiki* wins shows wherever it goes.

A chromed 324 Oldsmobile V-8, a narrowed '56 Olds dashboard, and a lot of show rod attitude add up to a distinctive ride.

The grille mesh, from a '58 Ford grille, is dotted with chrome drawer pulls. Headlight pods are the front 16 inches of 1960 Buick fenders. They were sectioned and pie-cut to get the right shape and size. Two 1936 Dodge headlight buckets form the backs of the headlight pods.

The engine once belonged to customizing pioneer, Joe Bailon, and three Stromberg carbs send fuel to it. Ignition is by a rare Grant Spaulding Flamethrower distributor. The tranny is a three-speed from a 1948 Ford truck.

Did You Know?

El Tiki was done completely in-house at Culbertson's Rods & Customs. Even the upholsterer came to the shop to do his work. The narrowed 1956 Olds dashboard wears patterned aluminum in the center that was taken from the interior of a 1960 Cadillac hearse. Round steel tubing was used to form the interior tub.

In late 1952, Detroit area butcher Marty Ribits acquired a somewhat rusty and beat-up 1934 Ford cabriolet. Ribits took the Ford to Bill Hines' shop, and the two laid out plans for the car. The body was channeled 6 inches, and other body components were adjusted so that the proportions remained aesthetically correct. That included sectioning the grille 6 inches. Custom rocker panels cover the channeling. The rear tail panel under the trunk lid was sectioned by 3½ inches, and the rear fenders were moved up the same amount. The car was painted a rich burgundy.

1934 FORD CABRIOLET GOLDEN NUGGET

Owner: Larry Jordon
Builder: Bill Hines/Larry Jordon
Engine: 1956 Buick Nailhead V-8
Photographer: Alan Mayes

At that time, Marty's '34 had a Mercury flathead with three deuces. It had a beautiful black-and-white, rolled-and-pleated interior done by a local upholsterer named Curly. The front end was reworked a little, extending the fenders behind the

bumper. Hines formed a custom pan that blended with the fenders and extended to the bumper. The car appeared in the August 1955 issue of *Car Craft* magazine in that form.

In 1956, Ribits purchased a new Buick Nailhead V-8 and installed it in place of the flathead. After a short period of wearing green paint, the '34 returned to Bill Hines' Custom Shop and emerged as the *Golden Nugget* with new metallic gold and clear lacquer. It then went on to win the first-place trophy for Altered Street Roadster at the 1958 Detroit Autorama.

Over the ensuing years, other interests and other cars eventually supplanted the '34, and it wound up sitting in a field.

Custom fan Larry Jordon and Ribits became friends, and Larry often tried to buy Marty's slowly deteriorating custom masterpiece but to no avail. A few years ago, Marty became terminally ill and willed the *Golden Nugget* to his nephew, Ray Lovasz. Marty's one stipulation in willing the '34 to Ray was that if Ray decided not to restore the car, he would pass the car on to Larry Jordon. Three years later, Ray passed it to Larry.

Larry soon found that a complete bare-metal restoration and replacement of many of the body panels were in store. Jordon took scrupulous measurements of every part of the car before starting disassembly.

One cannot appreciate the amount of work and the extensive modifications that Bill Hines put into the *Golden Nugget* and that Larry Jordon had to replicate. Jordon's reverence for the car and its original builder, and the desire to retain its heritage, came into play several times as he was restoring it.

The *Golden Nugget*'s restoration was finished in time for the 2005 Autorama, where Bill Hines was honored as Builder of the Year. Jordon was bestowed the Meguiar's Preservation Award for his efforts.

Did You Know?

The slightly hooded rims of the 1955 Chevy headlights were grafted onto many custom cars of the day, but builder Bill Hines took a different approach on the *Golden Nugget*. He turned the headlight housings upside down and tunneled them into the Ford's fenders, Pierce-Arrow style.

In addition to being an Ed "Big Daddy" Roth fan, Fritz Schenck is also a Roth purist, so when he set out to build a clone of the *Outlaw*, he was very meticulous in making sure he did things the way that Ed originally did them.

Starting with Model A frame rails, "the same as Roth did," Fritz set out to duplicate

FRITZ SCHENCK'S *OUTLAW* CLONE

Owner: Fritz Schenck
Builder: Fritz Schenck
Engine: 1950 Cadillac 331
Photographer: Alan Mayes

the *Outlaw*. He used a fiberglass body from Jimmy C., molded from a pattern taken from the original car's mold, and attached a highly modified 1922 Dodge windshield assembly. The nose piece was also provided by Jimmy C.

The original *Outlaw* was painted in 1959 by up-and-coming Larry Watson, who soon became one of the most sought-after custom painters of all time. Fritz painted his own but followed Watson's pattern exactly, using House of Kolor materials. It's pearl white with teal over silver panels. The taillights are twin housings from a 1958 Chevy Biscayne or Bel Air but with 1956 Chevy lenses.

The engine is a 1950 Cadillac 331 topped by a rare Cragar intake and Stromberg 97 carbs. The exhaust is homemade. Extensive chrome was applied throughout. The 1939 Ford three-speed transmission connects to a chrome-plated 1941 Ford rear end. Sitting atop the transmission is a Civil War sword handle shifter. That's a throwback to the original name of the Roth's *Outlaw*, *Excaliber*, and its first shifter.

The suspension for *Outlaw* includes a set of 1954 Chevy front coils over a Ford V-8-60 tube axle in front. The Ford rear end hangs on chrome Model A leaf springs. Front wheels are dragster spokes, and the rears are chromed 1951 Mercury wheels.

Did You Know?

The *Outlaw* interior includes a bench seat made from scrap plywood, topped with properly contoured foam, and covered in pearl-white vinyl and 1959 Pontiac teal vinyl at Trek Automotive in Huntington Station, New York. The steering wheel is from a 1958 Impala, and gauges are vintage Stewart-Warner large-logo style.

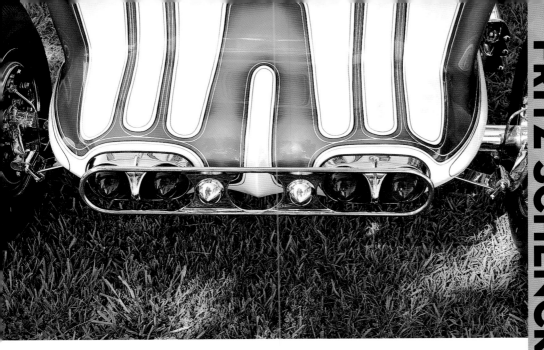

Completed in 1951, the *Skylane Motor Special* was named *Motor Trend*'s Convertible of the Year, and adorned the magazine's June 1951 cover. The *SMS* was built by Leroy J. Viersen Jr., with assistance from his son, Leroy III. The current owners are John and Angela Crego. Angela is the great-granddaughter of Leroy Jr. The *Skylane Motor Special* got its name from the Evinrude outboard motor business that Mr. Viersen owned and operated: Skylane Motor Parts in Sun Valley, California.

You would never know by looking at it, but the car was built on a 1932 Ford V-8 chassis. The rear was Z'ed and a '36 Ford rear end installed. Viersen used a 1940 Ford crossmember and custom adjustable

1951 SKYLANE MOTOR SPECIAL

Owner: John and Angela Crego
Builder: Leroy Viersen Jr. and Leroy Viersen III
Engine: 1948 Mercury
Photographer: Alan Mayes

wishbones to locate a '46 Mercury front axle. Motor mounts hold a '48 Mercury engine back 4 inches rearward of the original position.

Leroy Viersen Jr. wrote the following description of the car's body in a letter to *Motor Trend* in March 1951:

"The front fender and lights are 1948 Buick. The rear fenders and skirts are

1948 Lincoln Continental, altered to accommodate 1950 Oldsmobile taillights. Front and rear bumpers are 1950 Mercury. The grille is a 1949 Cadillac.

"The framework of the body was hand-formed from ³/8-inch pipe and welded together. The body was formed from 19-gauge sheet body steel. The body and fenders are all welded together, then hammer-welded, and hand-formed, making it a seamless one-piece body.

"The car has a wheelbase of 100 inches. It is 36 inches high at the cowl and 48 inches high at the top of the windshield."

According to surviving family members, concrete floors, sandbags, and hammers were the main tools used for building the car. When John Crego and Bobby Regeirro of Bob's Restoration in Los Angeles set about restoring the *SMS* a few years ago, there was the expected rust, but the workmanship was intact and nearly flawless.

Did You Know?

The engine on the *Skylane Motor Special* received state-of-the-art speed equipment for the day, equipment that is highly sought after today. It has a ³/4-grind camshaft and a custom-built Kong ignition with manual advance. An original Eddie Meyer dual manifold stands between Meyer heads.

One of Ed "Big Daddy" Roth's lesser-remembered customs was a single-seat hauler and accompanying motorcycle that was finished in 1967. Named *Mega Cycle*, the car's body was hand-built of fiberglass. It sat on a rectangular perimeter tube frame. Powered by a 1965 Buick V-6, it had a widened Corvair front suspension and a 1957 Chevy rear end. The car had a GM three-speed transmission and Cragar S/S wheels. It's a single-seater with a seat that conforms to the driver's body.

ED "BIG DADDY" ROTH'S MEGA CYCLE

Owner: Fritz Schenck
Builder: Ed "Big Daddy" Roth
Engine: 1965 Buick V-6
Photographer: Carrol Schenck

Over the years, *Mega Cycle* passed through several owners but finally wound up with Fritz Schenck of Spritz by Fritz in Belton, Missouri. Fritz has a reverence for the work

of Ed Roth and determined that *Mega Cycle* needed to be properly restored.

Matching paint on old customs is sometimes difficult because the cars are painted many times over, paint fades, and color pictures are hard to come by or are inaccurate when it comes to color hues. Thanks to some close observation, computer color matching, and luck, Fritz was able to match the color: a sky blue metalflake on one side and the same color on the other side but covered with candy blue.

The Triumph that rests with *Mega Cycle* wasn't originally with the car when it was built. Roth built the car to accept his Harley XLCH, but he later traded that to Bob Aquistapace for a show Triumph. Fritz is a long-time motorcycle builder and painter too, so he handled restoration of the bike with skill.

Did You Know?

Fritz Schenck is an accomplished custom builder and painter. He painted several of the late Indian Larry's custom motorcycles featured in magazines and on TV. He was also chosen by House of Kolor for one of their Top Ten Prestigious Painter Awards in 2009 and 2010.

CHAPTER 3
RAT RODS

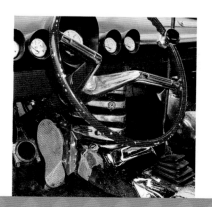

Cars defined as rat rods make up probably the single most polarizing category to ever enter the realm of hot rods. Their wildfire-like spread and acceptance have taken the rodding world by storm, pulling new fans in and alienating some old-time hot rodders at the same time.

Although some of the milder rat rods are similar in appearance to what were once called beaters or jalopies, the more radical vehicles are a game unto themselves. The term "rat rod" was originally coined as a derogatory distinction, but it has since gained acceptance as a general term, though certainly not an easily defined one.

It's somewhat humorous that several individuals claim to have coined the term or built and owned the cars that started the trend. As far as the name goes, who knows? And how would we be able to tell? As far as the cars themselves, the cars that some people claim to have started the trend are no different than cars that have been running around hot rod circles for 50 years—bare-bones, primered cars with a little road wear, some dust, and maybe a few dents; in other words, hot rods that have been on the road awhile and driven hard. Look in any of Albert Drake's excellent books chronicling the early days of hot rods, and you'll see the same cars. Those are traditional hot rods, like the more well-worn cars in Chapter 1 of this book.

Rat rods of today have transcended the traditional hot rod category and have become somewhat of an art form. Some owners at one end of the spectrum think that any vehicle (even a '94 Chevy S-10) that's in primer or rusty is a rat rod. Those people are wrong. The other end of the range goes to great effort to create a one-of-a-kind car that is sometimes barely drivable. Open, ear-level exhausts; rust (sometimes even "helped along" by applying salt water to the bare body); severely chopped roofs; missing windows; floorboards full of holes; and uncomfortable seats are the norm at the radical end of the spectrum. Mad Max would be afraid to ride in some of these cars. In this chapter, we have attempted to present a cross-section of the different types of cars commonly referred to as rat rods.

Probably 90 percent of the cars called rat rods today have either Model A Ford bodies or 1930s to 1940s pickup truck bodies. The reasons are simple enough.

In the car's four-year run from 1928 through 1931, there were nearly five million Model A Fords built, and an amazing number of them have survived to some extent. There may still be a few thousand (who knows the real number?) Model A bodies sitting in barns and fields and dry western ravines. Even pieces

of bodies can be put together to make a complete body, especially if Frankenstein welds are not a deterrent.

Old pickup truck bodies, some still on their frames, abound as well. In the days that those trucks were in use, trucks were workhorses. They were used on farms or as delivery or service vehicles and kept in reasonably good shape by mechanically minded farmers and business owners who literally used them until they wouldn't run any longer. Then they parked them.

Some are still sitting where they were parked decades ago, just waiting to become part of a rat rod. Coupes from the 1920s through 1940s have become too expensive for many rodders to afford. Pickup bodies have become the coupes of the new millennium.

Of the 12 rat rods in this chapter, there are four pickup bodies, five Model A's (one that was originally a sedan but has been made into a pickup), two Model T's, an Austin-Healey Sprite gasser, and a '34 Ford that maybe should have been in Chapter 1. It fits most people's criteria for a rat rod, though, so here it resides.

A quick perusal of the cars in this chapter will help illustrate just how ridiculously confusing this whole rat rod thing is. There are some pretty darned cool cars here, and several of them are not "ratty" at all, yet their owners built them to be rat rods by today's vernacular. Then there's that '34 cabriolet, which probably would have been a beater 30 years ago.

Aaron Mann's 1934 Ford cabriolet is a true old-school hot rod if there ever was one. Except for a few maintenance-related improvements, the car is virtually untouched from when it was built almost 50 years ago.

When Indianapolis resident, Joe Bastian, bought the '34 in 1959, it was already a hot rod with a flathead Ford powerplant and a straight axle with split wishbones. The body had been channeled 6 inches too.

Joe was a drag racer in the early 1960s, campaigning a 1960 Corvette with a 1956 265 V-8 bored out to 283. It had a '57 Corvette fuel injection and a Borg-Warner T-10 close-ratio four-speed. You guessed it. He transplanted the mechanicals from the Corvette to the Ford.

A 1961 Corvair Spyder donated its suspension, and a Corvair Greenbrier van gave up its steering box and column. The Posi-Traction rear end in the car came out of a 1960 Chevrolet and runs 4.56 gears.

Joe grabbed a set of Corvair bucket seats too. A 1960 Oldsmobile steering wheel sits on the Greenbrier column, and the speedometer is from a Checker cab. Rather than cut up the instrument panel

for gauges, Bastian made mounts to allow them to either float inside or behind the existing holes.

The car also has a custom rear bumper and a filled cowl vent. When the body was channeled over the frame, the rear quarters and wheelwells were massaged accordingly. The rear fenders and gas tank cover are bobbed originals.

That Chevy engine is pretty healthy, sporting 10.5 to 1 pistons and 1961 fuel injection heads, along with a Duntov cam. It has a rare W&H DuCoil ignition, an aluminum flywheel, and a hydraulic clutch.

1934 FORD CABRIOLET
Owner: Aaron Mann
Builder: Joe Bastian
Engine: 1956 Corvette 265 V-8
Photographer: Alan Mayes

Did You Know?
The front fenders and running boards on Aaron Mann's '34 are fiberglass but homemade. The originals from this very car were used as molds, and new ones were laid up by hand. The convertible top on the '34 was purchased from Montgomery Ward (remember them?).

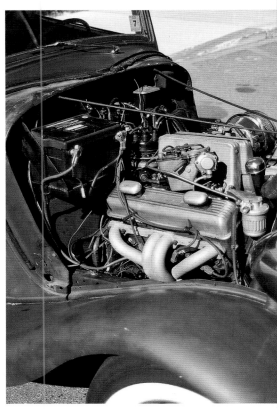

David Coker, owner of Newstalgia Wheel, headquartered in Chattanooga, Tennessee, went to the guys at Gas Monkey Garage in Texas when he was ready for a "new" company car. Aaron Kaufman was in charge of the project at Gas Monkey, and he and David worked closely to make sure there would be no mistaking the hardcore intent of David's ride. Gas Monkey Garage is famous for turning out radical, slammed hot rods with the accent on "hot."

David Coker wanted a head-turning rat rod but one that was dependable and could be driven relatively comfortably whenever he took the notion to do so. The chassis includes a very solid 2x4-inch tubular frame that was Z'ed 6 inches in the front and 12 inches in the back. It drops to the ground with custom air bags in the front and the rear. The front rides on a Super Bell dropped I-beam axle with split stock wishbones. This baby can get low!

Once Coker rolls into the cabin through door about waist high, the environs are really pretty comfy. The leather seat cushions are on the floor, which gives a legs-straight-out seating position. Back cushions are leather too, and they're mounted to the structure that covers all the mechanical workings of the air ride and the deeply Z'ed frame. Grass mats cover the floor and the box structure. Mounted atop the box is a Vintage Air underdash unit that faces forward.

1931 FORD SEDAN

Owner: David Coker
Builder: Gas Monkey Garage
Engine: ZZ4 Chevy 350 crate engine
Photographer: Alan Mayes

Did You Know?

A hot rod has one major purpose: go like stink. This one can accommodate with its 430-horsepower ZZ4 Chevy 350 with a hot hydraulic roller cam. An Offenhauser manifold with a 670 Holley sits atop the engine. That's all backed by a 700R4 overdrive tranny. Overdrive for economy. Right.

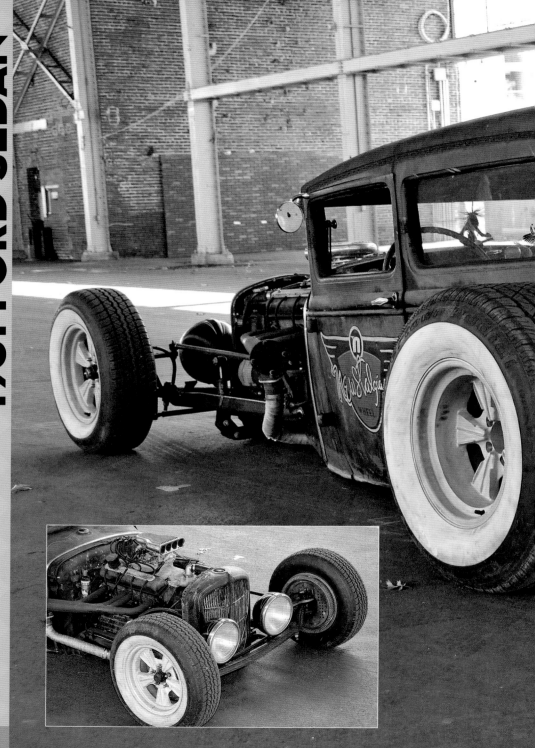

1931 FORD SEDAN

Toolmakers apply the close tolerances they use in their everyday jobs to the building of their cars, and the result is usually a very special car. Here's one of those cars by one of those guys, toolmaker Dave Thomson.

"Being a [toolmaker], I tried to make everything I could or fabricate parts out of other things rather than just buying a

1926 FORD COUPE

Owner: Dave Thomson
Builder: Dave Thomson
Engine: 1974 Mazda four-cylinder
Photographer: Jimmy Faris

iece off the shelf," Thomson said. "I used flexible copper water heater supply line for conduit, headlight buckets for gauge pods, and friction shock pieces for the brake and clutch pedals."

The engine for this car is unusual, a Mazda four-cylinder from a 1974 Ford Courier pickup. Its exhaust note is very distinctive for an inline four-cylinder. That's because the Mazda engine came stock from the factory with a split exhaust manifold. Dave simply added a set of Speedway megaphones. A Holley 94 carb was added to the stock intake manifold.

"The four-cylinder just made sense," Dave said. "Not only is it reliable, its light weight helps with the way the car handles, not to mention the good gas mileage."

The car is built for low maintenance with its Mexican blanket over a Dodge van seat and flat-brown exterior. Front suspension is a '46 Ford axle on split wishbones and a transverse spring. The '46 Ford rear is also on a transverse spring. The 1940s Ford suspension and brake parts are more than heavy-duty enough for a lightweight Model T, and reproduction parts are plentiful. Good planning by the toolmaker.

Did You Know?

Dave Thomson calls his car *Cut Down*. He noticed, while thumbing through some hot rodding magazines from the 1950s for some ideas, that the phrase was used to describe a chopped Model T. So, Dave adopted the term and made it the name of his Model T.

1926 FORD COUPE

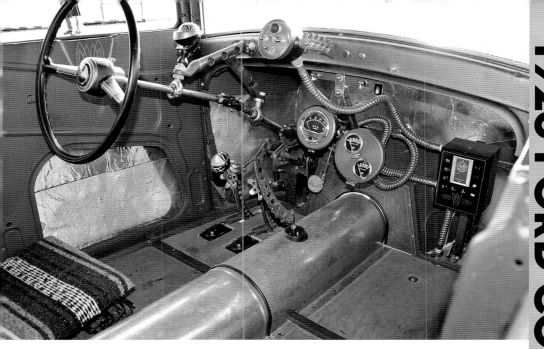

Dubbed *Fubar Pillbox*, Danny O'Neill's military-themed 1925 Ford pickup was a yearlong project. Finished the night before the 2008 Rat City Rukkus in Las Vegas, it won Best in Show at that first outing.

Inspired by Danny's friend, Jim Boykins, who is a World War II veteran, the *Pillbox* is not a tank, but it's built like one. It sits on a custom tubular frame crafted by Bobby Masterson and Smokin' Joe Dearborn. An 8-inch Ford rear end was shortened 3 inches.

1925 FORD PICKUP

Owner: Danny O'Neill
Builder: Danny O'Neill
Engine: 1968 302 Ford
Photographer: Anna Marco

A four-link ladder bar suspension with 8-inch air bags adjusts the truck's height for desert running or city work.

A 1968 302 Ford motor with ceramic-coated headers, an Offenhauser high-rise intake, and an Edelbrock 650 carb gives sufficient power. A 32-inch, double-bend Lokar shifter with a genuine World War II hand grenade grip sits atop a Ford C4 transmission.

Inside the truck bed are an 11-gallon spun-aluminum gas tank, ammo box for emergency gear, and spare gas tank. Danny says that the floorboards and bed were handmade with the help of Will Blomster and Scott Evans at Universal Metals in Las Vegas.

The interior is pretty spartan, which follows the theme. Olive drab sheet metal abounds, and an ammo box serves as center console. Throughout the vehicle, the military detailing is remarkably authentic. O'Neill did his homework at the local library.

Did You Know?

This truck was chopped 18 inches and then channeled an additional 6 inches. It sits low! The windows are like slits. The two smallest ones are designed like gun turrets. The PPG Army Green etching primer and military insignias by Eddie Brown are period correct.

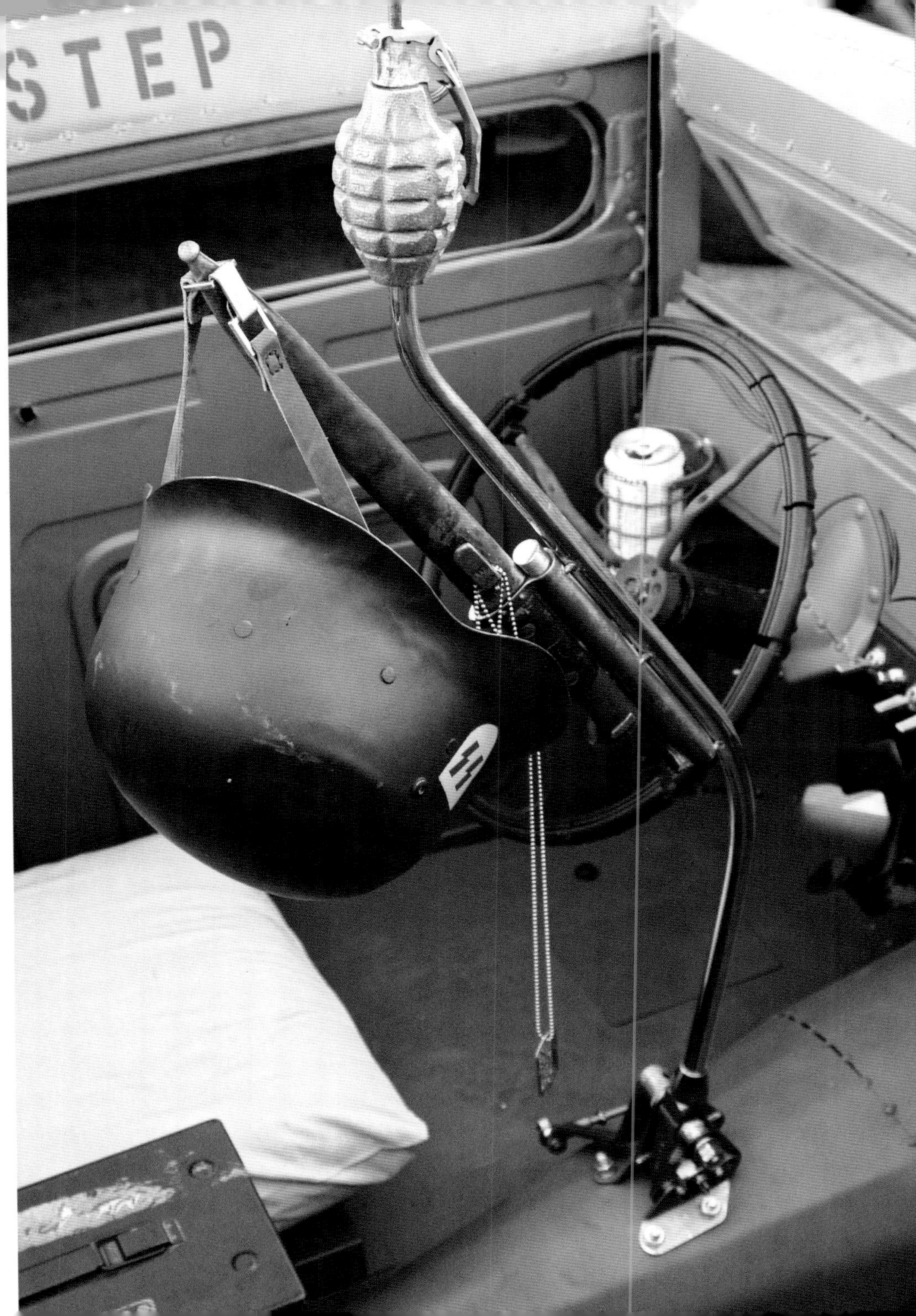
STEP

Looking at this car up close, it's easy to see that it's well-built, so it's safe and dependable to drive. But it's also obvious from the dust, a few scratches, and a little bit of rust showing on the suspension pieces that it's not a trailer queen show car. It's a hot rod, driven by Lou Lewis on the mean streets of Indianapolis.

The roadster was originally built around 1970 as a highboy by Gary Monday, a friend of Lou's dad. Lou found it in the late 1990s. He bought the car and stored it away for a few years. When he finally started to work on the car, he threw the old frame away and had a new frame built.

Lou Lewis then rebuilt the car, completing it in 2006. That includes a rebuilt 350 Chevy engine, which was bored 0.030 inch over in the process. Intake chores are handled by a very desirable Fenton

tri-power with Rochester 2G carburetors. A Turbo 350 transmission gets power connected to the 1957 Chevy rear end. The rest of the running gear follows the same traditional theme: chrome reverse wheels, a Ford dropped axle with drum brakes, and chrome hairpins.

The paint job is a simple as it gets—Krylon flat black from a spray can. Pinstriping and lettering are courtesy of Little Bill.

1929 FORD ROADSTER

Owner: Lou Lewis
Builder: Gary Monday/Lou Lewis
Engine: 1973 Chevy 350
Photographer: Craig Mayes

Did You Know?

Inside the cockpit of the 313 roadster, Stewart-Warner gauges and a '40 Chevy speedometer send info out from a stock dashboard. The seats are vinyl Dodge van buckets, and the "carpet" is really a Mexican blanket. The 313 name comes from the area code for Detroit's telephone exchange.

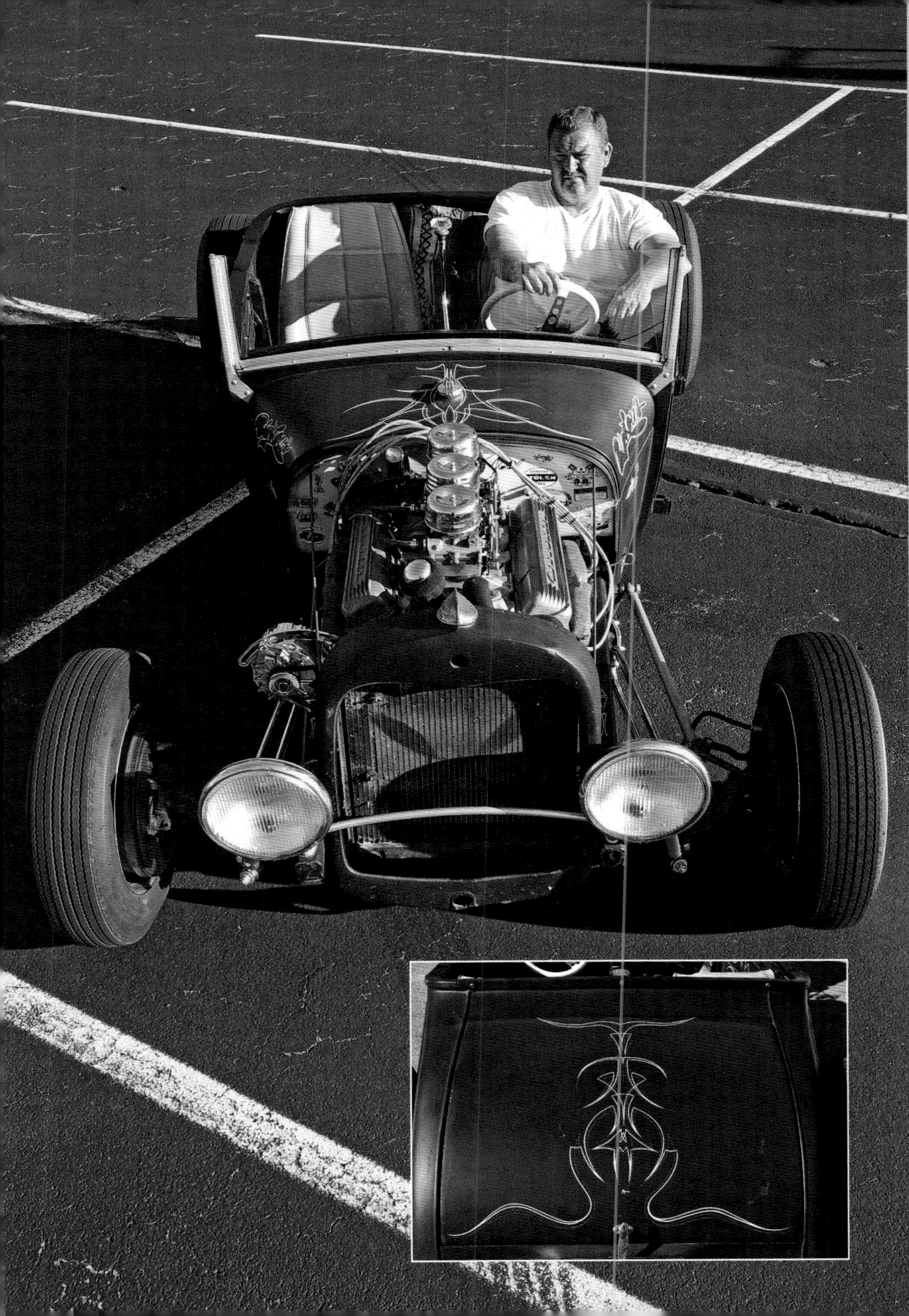

Sammy Vildosola of Laguna Hills, California, has been fabricating since the early 1960s. His early creations were sand rails and drag cars, but lately he's been doing hot rods, which are what most folks call rat rods. Closer examination of the photos will reveal that there is nothing ratty about the construction quality, though. The chassis of Sammy's cars are built to his drag car standards—safe and highly roadworthy. Most of his cars are sold before they're finished. They go all over the place, including Japan.

1929 FORD ROADSTER

Owner: Sammy Vildosola
Builder: Sammy Vildosola
Engine: 1968 Chevy 350
Photographer: Anna Marco

This particular roadster spends a lot of time on the highway and gets its power from a 1968 Chevy 350 engine backed by a Turbo 350 transmission with Mustang shifter. The megaphone-style headers and custom carb scoop are trademark Sammy parts. A 1964

Mustang radiator keeps the engine cool. The front axle and suspension are from a '40 Ford. Rear suspension on the '51 Mercury rear end is from a '32 Ford, and all the brakes started life on a '46 Ford.

The infamous Jimmy C. did the rat graphics on the red-oxide-primered doors. The steering column came from a 1958 VW bus. Bomber seats keep driver and passenger secure on hard turns. The front tires on the car are 5.10-16 motorcycle tires. Whitewall motorcycle tires have whitewalls on both sides, which works great on a fenderless

car. Sammy adapted a tilting Model T windshield to the car's cowl.

Did You Know?

This car looks like a Model A roadster now, but it didn't start out that way. As often happens these days, it started out as a more plentiful and less expensive sedan. Some deft cutting, grafting, and fabricating by owner and fabricator, Sammy Vildosola, made it into a roadster.

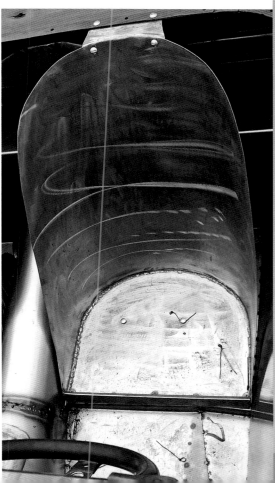

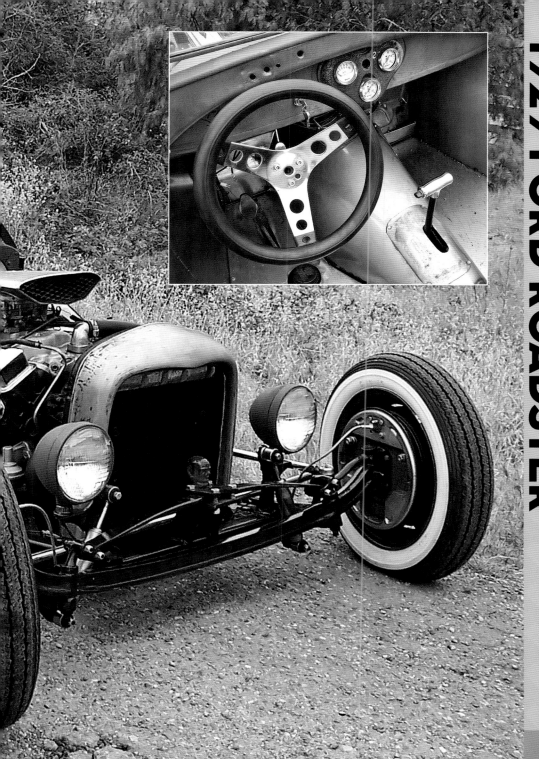

In 1964, the racing bug bit Bill Bierman Sr., as it did many a young man at that time. Already the owner of a big and powerful 348 Chevy engine with tri-power, he just needed a light car to stuff it in. The perfect candidate was owned by an acquaintance: a '59 Austin-Healey "Bugeye" Sprite.

The Sprite was already pointed in the drag racing direction with a VW beam axle, an Olds rear end, and ladder bars. Bill bought the car and raced it for many years, but family responsibilities forced him to sell it.

1959 AUSTIN-HEALEY SPRITE

Owner: Bill Bierman Sr.
Builder: Bill Bierman Jr.
Engine: 1959 Chevy 348
Photographer: Jimmy Faris

Forty years later, Bill's son, Bill Jr., owner of Creative Customs Auto Body in St. Louis, was looking for a car like his dad's, hoping to build a clone of that Sprite for his father. A friend found one on Craigslist, and the

same seller had a VW beam axle to go with it! Fate had intervened, and the project was underway. Friends and family pitched in to build, fabricate, and tell the necessary little white lies to keep Bill Sr. in the dark.

Bill Jr. decided to construct the car so that it had the appearance of a vehicle that had survived 40-plus years intact but well-used and slightly neglected. All Sprites are rusted, so he left some of the rust on the body. He painted the car green, sprayed orange over it, and hand-aged the finish with sandpaper.

The car was finished in time to present it to Bill Sr. on Father's Day at the NHRA Hot Rod Reunion in Bowling Green, Kentucky.

Did You Know?
This Sprite drag car is a replica of one owned by Bill Bierman Sr. many years ago. When he first saw the car, Bill thought they'd actually found the original Austin-Healey. Even the track announcer at the event mentioned that he remembered the Sprite from the good old days!

There's a whole lot more work involved in this car than you would first notice. See, it started out as a 1938 Dodge pickup truck. Colorado resident Chad Warne knew what he wanted for his first hot rod, and he was fortunate in having a rod builder, John Curtis, for a father-in-law.

Warne sketched out his dream hot rod and them tacked the sketches to the garage wall. Then he and Curtis built the car. A donated 1938 Ford frame serves as the foundation. It had to be modified to fit the Dodge body. The suspension consists of a

1938 DODGE ROADSTER

Owner: Chad Warne
Builder: Chad Warne/John Curtis
Engine: 1956 Chrysler 354 Hemi
Photographer: Roger Jetter

triangulated four-link in the rear supporting a 9-inch Lincoln Versailles disc brake rear end. In front, a Super Bell 4-inch-dropped axle, spindles, and hairpins were used. A 1956 Chrysler Hemi provides the power for the car.

The top of the Dodge truck cab was cut off, and the windshield was chopped 3½ inches. The truck bed went in the dumpster too. Chad's idea for his dream rod included a narrowed 1956 Chrysler tail section. A four-door sedan was the donor car. The Chrysler rear and bumper had to be narrowed 15 inches to work. It was then mated to the truck cab and channeled 5 inches over the frame. To make everything look cohesive, the Chrysler body lines were extended into the truck cab.

Did You Know?

The interior of Chad Warne's truck received a lot of attention. A 1951 Buick instrument panel was narrowed, and Buick door panels were molded to fit the doors. A Buick steering column was installed and topped with a custom wheel using the Buick horn ring. The seat is from a Dodge van.

At first glance, most people have a hard time figuring out what kind of truck this is. That's understandable, because the 1937 Hudson Terraplane nose is obviously on a truck that is not a '37 Terraplane. The cab is not much help, either, because it is far from stock. Most people give up and just ask. It's a 1946 Chevy, chopped 6 inches, with a laid-back windshield and the upper parts of the doors removed.

Indiana's Ted Houchin originally built this critically acclaimed truck (receiving awards at Detroit Autorama from both Chip Foose and Troy Trepenier), but it now belongs to Bob Sargis of Louisville, Kentucky.

It features six Stromberg carbs atop a 1958 364-cubic-inch Buick Nailhead V-8 and a magneto ignition. The frame was custom built from 2x3-inch tubing. Original Ford-style, 16-inch Kelsey-Hayes wire wheels

are utilized along with dirt-track-patterned Firestone and Excelsior tires from Coker Tire Company. The truck bed began life on a Model A Ford.

The truck's original 1946 Chevy grille didn't go to waste when it was replaced by the Terraplane piece. The Chevy grille was cut way down and sits below the dashboard and above a chrome oil pan used for the shifter console. There's a connecting rod

brake pedal and a foot gas pedal. A 1960 Oldsmobile steering wheel, Chevy Impala gauges, and Indian blanket upholstery finish off the interior.

1946 CHEVROLET PICKUP

Owner: Bob Sargis
Builder: Ted Houchin
Engine: 1958 Buick 364 Nailhead V-8
Photographer: Anna Marco

Did You Know?

Those large headlights on the front of this truck feature accessory Stabilite lenses from Brown Manufacturing Company in Cincinnati, Ohio. They were a popular 1930s accessory lens upgrade, appearing on many Packards, Cadillacs, and Lincolns of the period.

1946
DIDDLER
AWARD
WINNER

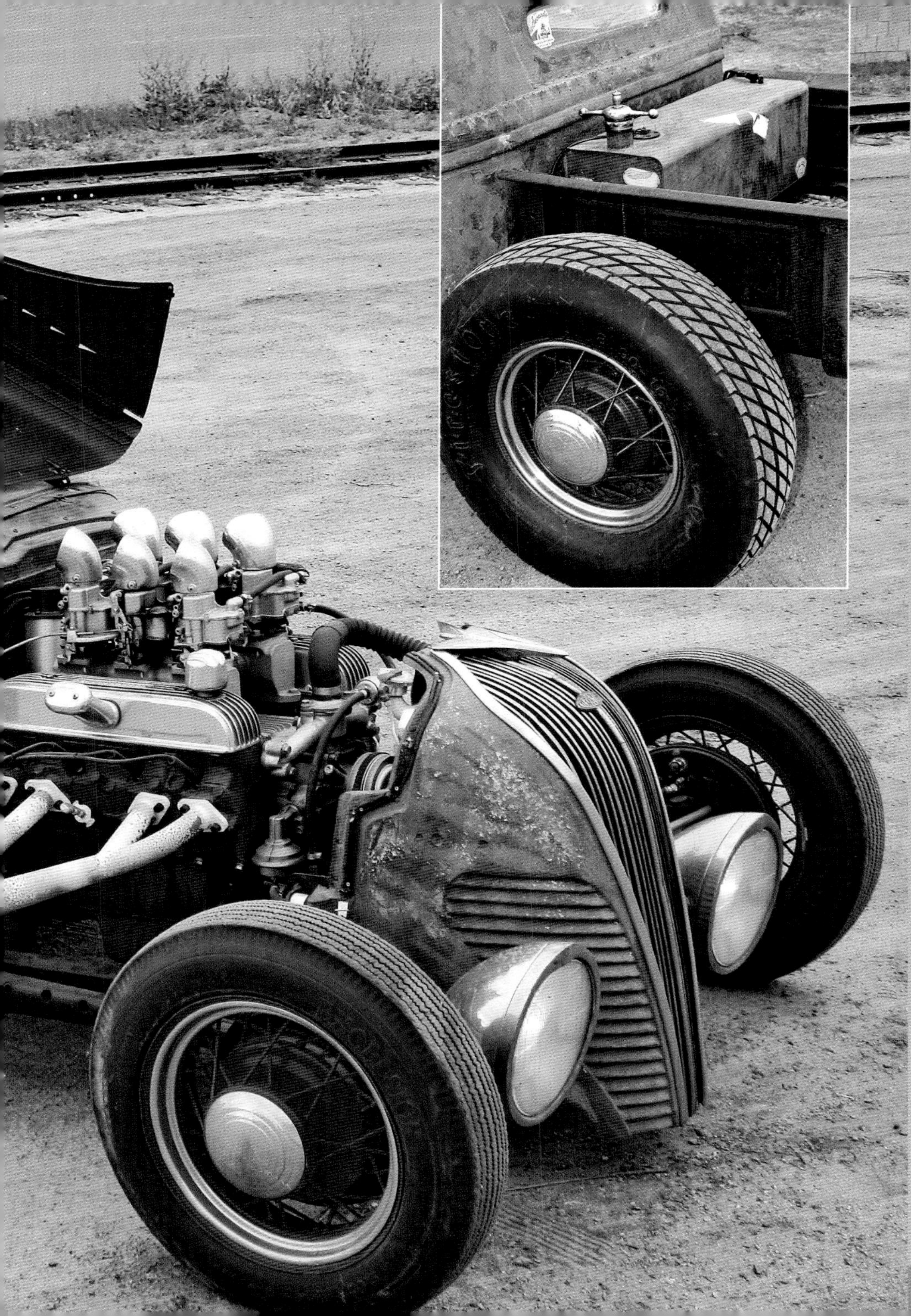

Barry Hilderbrand is an active member of the Odd Rods Car Club in Georgia, and he's also the owner and builder of this exceptional 1935 Ford Victoria. Well, more of a Victoria-ette, actually. It's been shortened 12 inches, so it's more of a long coupe with no trunk. When you combine that with a raised rear end and a top chopped 4½ inches, and place it on big and little tires, you get one fine raked hot rod.

This hot rod is powered by a 1967 Chevy 327 with 400 horsepower blowing out through hand-formed long zoomie headers. The car is very roadworthy with its five-speed overdrive manual tranny. And taking it on the road is exactly what Barry does. He reports that he drove it 10,000 miles last year. He's a firm believer in the "hot rods should be driven" philosophy.

Since the car is a driver, Barry opted for some pretty plush black leather bucket seats. There's nothing wrong with being comfy, and it's one thing that separates a fun, drivable car

from one that's a chore to drive. Roll-beaded aluminum side panels and a stock '35 dashed filled with Stewart-Warner Wings gauges nicely finish off the interior.

Adding to the driving pleasure, the aforementioned big and little tires are radials for better grip and handling. Safe stopping is at least as important as going, probably more so, and that chore is covered well with regular cast-iron drums in back and finned Buick drums in front.

1935 FORD VICTORIA

Owner: Barry Hilderbrand
Builder: Barry Hilderbrand
Engine: 1967 Chevy 327
Photographer: Jack Criswell

Did You Know?

Barry Hilderbrand painted his 1935 Ford Victoria with Rustoleum paint, which is available at hardware and home improvement stores. Although it doesn't provide the shine of more expensive automotive paint, it's durable and inexpensive. It's a viable low-dollar alternative.

There's a lot of things that are unusual about this hot rod, not the least of which is that it's a right-hand-drive model. That's because it's from Australia, mate. Rod Hadfield and friends built this baby in one year.

The engine powering this car is kind of unusual hot rod fare too. Oh, it's a flathead all right, but a 1948 V-12 Lincoln variety with 50 percent more pistons and almost 50 percent more length too. That requires the wheelbase to be a bit longer as well, which adds to the ride comfort. Atop the V-12, you'll find a GM 653 blower and three Stromberg 97 carburetors. The vintage tranny has a fiberglass shifter custom cast to match Rod's hand, and it's holding a wrench. The interior is upholstered in burlap.

The suspension consists of a 1934 Ford front end and a 1948 Australian Ute

differential with a Model A spring in the rear. Fordson tractor headlights, front shocks, and the radiator are all mounted on one bracket. Twin coils and an English BMC 12-volt generator are used, as are original Model A taillights.

The truck's bed was shortened 3 inches and features hidden storage space under the bed. A legitimate Victoria license plate reads "RATROD."

1928 FORD PICKUP

Owner: Rod Hadfield
Builder: Rod Hadfield
Engine: 1948 Lincoln V-12
Photographer: Anna Marco

Did You Know?

Part of building a rat rod is pressing on-hand or cast-off items into service. Rod Hadfield used army jerry cans as fuel tanks and a 1942 petrol drum for spare oil. An original tool box is in the bed, which is lined with wooden slats.

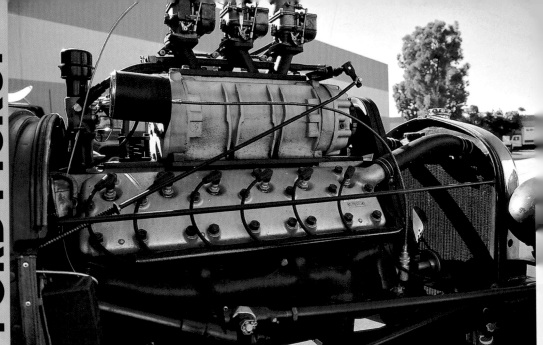

Aaron Hagar is the owner of Rat Runners Garage, a hot rod shop in Lake Tahoe that specializes, as the name implies, in rat rods. He's also a musician and an artist, a multitalented guy. Does the last name sound familiar? That's not surprising, since Aaron is the son of rock-'n'-roll legend Sammy Hagar. Aaron inherited Sammy's musical talent and his love for cars too. "I Can't Drive 55" is not just a song title! It's a family mantra.

World War II bomber nose art has always appealed to Aaron (what's not to like, right?),

so he used that as inspiration for his 1946 GMC–based rat rod. The pretty, redheaded pinups adorn both doors of the truck and inspire the name *Red Voodoo*. The interior door panels carry more pinup art, while the rest of the interior and other areas follow the bomber motif. That includes the use of vintage aircraft gauges and switches hung all over a 1951 DeSoto instrument panel, bomber seats, and compass.

This truck is a bit of a Frankenstein's monster, not unusual in the world of rat

rods. While the cab is from a 1946 GMC truck, it's from a larger truck (reportedly a Reno, Nevada, city tow truck), making the frame a little heavy-duty for runaround hot rod usage. So Aaron dropped the body on a 1938 Chevy chassis and added a bed from a 1953 Chevy pickup. The cab was chopped 4 inches and channeled about the same amount. Up front at the business end of the chassis can be found a Chevy 454 big-block engine connected to a Turbo 350 transmission.

1946 GMC PICKUP

Owner: Aaron Hagar
Builder: Aaron Hagar
Engine: 1970 Chevy 454
Photographers: Tom Gomez and Aaron Hagar

Did You Know?

This is definitely a themed truck. The interior of Aaron Hagar's GMC rat rod is furnished with genuine vintage World War II bomber pieces. Two styles of bomber seats with genuine safety harnesses face aircraft gauges and switches. Outside, the exhaust pipes are capped with tips from real tail-gunner mini barrels from a big-caliber machine gun.

INDEX